A True Story of Love, Loss, and Bold Living

Both Sides Now

Nancy Sharp

Books & Books Press

Praise for

Both Sides Now

"*Both Sides Now* is an unflinching memoir of love and loss and hope. Nancy Sharp's honesty and hard-earned wisdom make this book essential reading for anyone facing adversity—which is all of us."

— ANN HOOD, author of *Comfort*, *The Red Thread*, and *The Obituary Writer*

"Nancy Sharp's elegant, heartbreaking, life-affirming memoir is both a meditation on grief and a call to action. Having lost her husband to cancer while they were both in their thirties and been left with twin toddlers to bring up on her own, the author knows that paralysis was not an option, and thus she chronicles her journey of defiant healing. Written in a voice that is at some times as intimate as a lover's whisper and at others as clear and public and measured as a church bell pealing in the distance, Sharp's book grabs life by its tattered collar, examining the ambiguity and the complexity, the mess and the mystery. In the tradition of such classics as *A Grief Observed*, *Death Be Not Proud*, and *The Year of Magical Thinking*, *Both Sides Now* appears slated to join the rare but wondrous ranks of personal writing raised to the level of universal appeal."

— MADELEINE BLAIS, Pulitzer Prize winner and author of
Uphill Walkers: Memoir of a Family and *In These Girls, Hope Is a Muscle*

"The Nancy Sharp you will meet in this moving memoir is an exemplar of honesty, courage, and grace. I know of no other book that addresses the pain of loss and the challenge of recovery with the fierce intimacy displayed in *Both Sides Now*."

— DANIEL OKRENT, author, *Last Call:*
The Rise and Fall of Prohibition; former editor, *Life* magazine

"*Both Sides Now* is simultaneously devastating, inspiring, and moving. The true story resonates with the bittersweet tragicomedy that is life; at once too strange to be real, often funny, excruciating, and deeply romantic. Written by a courageous woman who has 'been there,' this book painstakingly makes the personal universal. She instills hope after loss, and gives us a literary primer on 'how to' survive when life hands you the unimaginable."

— SUSAN CARTSONIS, producer, *What Women Want,*
Where the Heart Is, Aquamarine, and *No Reservations*

"The immediacy, the candor, and the bravery of this book are impressive beyond even its devastating facts. Nancy Sharp's memoir gives new life to the phrase 'grace under pressure.'"

— RICHARD TODD, former magazine and book editor,
New England Monthly and *The Atlantic*; author of *The Thing Itself: On the Search for Authenticity*;
and coauthor with Tracy Kidder of *Good Prose: The Art of Nonfiction*

"What Nancy Sharp lost early in her adult life might have made her a realist of the wary sort, but that would have been too easy for this resilient and determined writer, whose life force was too strong for death. Sharp's language of loss is unafraid of mourning and dirge, so that when she moves from elegy to celebration, it feels hard-won, authentic, believable. Her writing opens first to hope and possibility, and then to the certainty of renewed delight. In her good company, we open to these gifts ourselves."

— DIANA HUME GEORGE, author of *The Lonely Other: A Woman Watching America*; codirector, Chautauqua Writers' Festival; contributing editor, *Chautauqua* journal; professor of English emerita, Penn State University

"The stars were on their side and then they weren't. In *Both Sides Now* Nancy Sharp unfolds the destruction of American optimism by a triple punch from horrific fate. She does it in such a transparent, direct way that the reader gets the benefit of the experience. This is a book in which you learn about life."

— SUZANNAH LESSARD, author of *The Architect of Desire: Beauty and Danger in the Stanford White Family* and the recently completed *The Absent Hand: A Meditation on the American Landscape*; former editor, *The Washington Times* and staff writer, *The New Yorker*

"This is a book about loss. But it is also a story about rebounding and the power of attitude. You can't help but cheer from the sidelines as Nancy Sharp builds a second life for herself and her young twins after her husband's premature death. Having survived two life-threatening bouts of cancer, I was very moved by the insights Sharp provides from the perspective of caregiver. *Both Sides Now* is a brave, inspiring story."

— GEORGE KARL, former head coach, Denver Nuggets; cancer survivor

"Nancy Sharp's story will break your heart while lifting you at the same time. This is an intimate portrait of one family that speaks to all of us because life and death are the purest parts of the human experience. Sharp takes us on a physical and spiritual journey, allowing us to think more reflectively about the choices we make in our own lives. This beautifully written book will teach you many things about strength, perseverance, and what it means to reach for the mountains."

—TERRIE M. WILLIAMS, author of *Black Pain: It Just Looks Like We're Not Hurting*, *The Personal Touch: What You Really Need to Succeed in Today's Fast Paced Business World*, and *A Plentiful Harvest: Creating Balance and Harmony Through the Seven Living Virtues*

"The surreal and dislocating nature of 'the first contact' with cancer never loses its potent sting; it is such a cruel disease to everyone it touches. Cancer may be relentless, but so are we, and even though there are no true wins or losses, we struggle on, as I believe this is fundamental to the nature of our humanity to fight for what's really important. Perhaps it's this terrible struggle that ultimately enables us to heal."

—DR. MICHAEL SISTI, James G. McMurtry, associate professor of clinical neurosurgery, radiation oncology, and otolaryngology; codirector, Center for Radiosurgery, Columbia University Medical Center

"Sharp's memoir, which is simultaneously understated and passionate in its expression, confronts the reader with the dualities of birth and death, love and loss, hope and despair. These universal forces are starkly evident in Sharp's portrayal of her twins, born prematurely into a world where their father is fighting for his life. The children's fierce attachment to their father in the not quite three years that they 'have' him, their bewilderment at his disappearance, and their spirited determination to keep him close in their lives infuse the narrative with a unique poignancy and power. The children's voices, rarely heard in the literature on 'living through loss,' remind us all of the resilience of hope and renewal in our lives."

—BARBARA M. SOURKES, PH.D., professor of pediatrics, Stanford University School of Medicine; John A. Kriewall and Elizabeth A. Haehl director, Pediatric Palliative Care, Lucile Packard Children's Hospital at Stanford

"Thank you, Nancy Sharp, for this gift. Your brilliant writing compels the reader to acutely feel your love, shock, pain, hope, and resolve. We are right there with you and your beautiful family on the journey and cheer as you show up, participate, and grab at life as though it's your last day. Once I was your Rabbi. In this wonderful book you are mine."

—RABBI ROBERT LEVINE, senior rabbi, Congregation Rodeph Sholom; author of *What God Can Do for You Now: For Seekers Who Want to Believe* and *Where Are You When I Need You? Befriending God When Life Hurts*

"Nancy Sharp's *Both Sides Now* adds another verse to Joni Mitchell's classic song. Love's illusion is resolved in this courageous tribute to loss and living on. A young widow with twin toddlers in tow and grief's mud caked in her soul picks herself up and heads west. The open sky beckons. She looks heavenward and feels the presence of her beloved Brett and shakes off the mud to breathe in new life. In the words of the Psalms, 'Those who sow in tears will reap in joy.' Sharp takes us through all the seasons. Hers is a factual tale of two cities and an inspiring tale of two loves."

— DR. DAVID SANDERS, clinical psychologist and founder and director of Kabbalah Experience; author of *Neshama: The Journey of the Soul*; and coauthor with Martin Mendelsberg of *Eternal Letters*

"Nancy Sharp's book, *Both Sides Now*, is a soaring story of one woman's journey through love and loss and back to love again. The writing is heartbreaking and ultimately full of hope—part confession and part prayer, with emotions so raw and honest that the reader can't help but share her sorrows and rejoice at the end of the tunnel. *Both Sides Now* is a book for anyone who needs strength to come into the light from a very dark place."

— VICKY COLLINS, Emmy Award winning television producer; president, Teletrends Television Production and Development

"Nancy Sharp tells a story of life in a story of death. After you discover all she lost and, then, found again, you will hug your children, husband, wife, family, and friends an extra time or two."

— WALT HARRINGTON, author of *The Everlasting Stream*, *The Beholder's Eye*, *Crossings*, and *Intimate Journalism*

"This is not merely one of those 'one-day' books that we all love to love—a book so gripping and moving and fleet of foot that the ending won't wait for tomorrow. Instead, Nancy Sharp transmutes a shocking story of love and loss into a work of literature that rewards rereading, one that ruminates on life, death, and everything in between with a poet's sensitivity to language, a psychologist's grasp of complicated emotions, and a wife's and mother's sense of unbounded love."

— JONATHAN GILL, author of *Harlem: The Four Hundred Year History from Dutch Village to Capital of Black America*; professor of American literature and history, University of Amsterdam

for Rebecca and Casey —

The Sky Is Everywhere

Were it possible for us to see further than our knowledge reaches, and yet a little way beyond the outworks of our divining, perhaps we would endure our sadnesses with greater confidence than our joys. For they are the moments when something new has entered into us, something unknown; our feelings grow mute in shy perplexity, everything in us withdraws, a stillness comes, and the new, whichno one knows, stands in the midst of it and is silent.

RAINER MARIA RILKE

Author's Note

BOTH SIDES NOW IS A WORK OF NONFICTION. The events, people, and facts depicted here are real. To write the story, I relied upon medical records, personal journals, research, interviews with people featured in these pages (and many not), and of course, my own memory. Sometimes I found myself triple-checking dates to be sure I'd gotten them right, such was the frailty of my working memory following my first husband's cancer diagnosis. It goes without saying that while no composite characters or moments exist in the book, I opted to include only those scenes that heightened the narrative. Over time, I discovered the truest way for me to render grief was to use short chapters—fragments that mirror the way people tend to cope—allowing necessary breathing space for myself, and readers. It's my hope that this book can be a bridge for those who have struggled to move beyond mourning toward life again, past and present at one.

Prologue

NOVEMBER 2004. I sat among a small group of strangers at Rodeph Sholom Synagogue on the Upper West Side. I wasn't praying. I was grieving.

Everyone noticed that I was the youngest person by decades in this bereavement group. I was aware of them seeing me, a young woman, wondering, *Why is she here?* Sad as they appeared over their own losses, they looked at me with pity. No one asked my age, not at first. As my eyes searched the room, landing upon one gray-flecked head after another, I felt the oddity of being in this situation: young and old at the same time. I didn't want their pity. I didn't want anyone's pity. I only wanted to feel better.

I listened to their stories—tales of long love, children, grand-children, memories of museum outings, bike vacations, and retirement dreams cut short. The room was a sea of bereft voices. *What was I doing here?* I began to tap my heel on the carpet, thinking about the toast my son threw this morning while his twin sister banged the back of her head against the floor. They were three and a half years old. We were working on potty training. I was fixed on these thoughts, restless to return home, when Ben, who sat across from me, snapped me out of it. A few times he opened his mouth to speak, then shut it, unable to find the words. He was in awful pain, crying with his eyes closed and gently pressing the tips of his long fingers together for comfort. His thin, white hair was askew.

Ben was ninety-seven years old, mourning his wife of more than sixty years. I was thirty-eight years old, mourning my husband, Brett, who had died a few months shy of his fortieth birthday.

Ben's griefs were tangled together like fishing line; he mourned his wife, and his own end, which he expected soon. He still lived at home. Alone. Every strained feature of his face suggested that he'd given up on living. What was the point? What kind of future could he really welcome? Some days I feared Ben might will himself to die in the room. If he did, at least he would be with people who understood. *Did any of us really understand?*

I began to feel closer to Ben. Frail as he was, his spirit obviously needed healing. Why else would he be here? It was true that he mourned everything at once. And the question of mortality, which every surviving spouse, young and aged, contemplates, was real for Ben in a way it wasn't for me. Life can end at any point, there are no guarantees, but a man nearing a hundred can have few illusions. This much was true: I would not have a future with my sweet husband; those dreams had died. But probably I would have *a* future. Even though I couldn't see it then, and was not yet able to grasp at anything concrete. *Wait a year* goes the common wisdom. Like Ben, I was thrown by all that had happened, but I couldn't give up on life at thirty-eight. I wouldn't do that to myself, and I wouldn't do it to my young children.

Ben shuffled his feet just like my grandfather. I felt protective of him, wanting to steady him with my arm since he used no cane. The trip here exhausted him, and each time he spoke, he cried. We became friends, and once I took him to a Shabbat service with my twins. It surprised me that being around him comforted me: his old age both separated us and drew me to him. Despite our differences, we felt a shared sense of brokenness. Besides, his name was my son's middle name—Ben, in memory of Brett's grandfather.

One day Ben brought all the women silver chains that his wife had made. He needed to share this offering, this relic of their lives;

he knew, even in these fresh moments of grief, the chains would hold up against time. The one he gave me had rows of identical circles and was the length of half a belt. I wrapped it around my wrist and wore it as a bracelet. All these years later, it remains a favorite possession.

I pictured Ben sitting on a floral couch next to his wife, a protective arm around her. She knew precisely where to lean her head against his chest; the soft spot, hers alone. Ben gave me hope for a long life.

It's the path I always saw for Brett and me—a long and certain life together. We married in our twenties, and because we had grown up in neighboring towns with parents still together and mutual friends of all ages, we shared an unspoken assumption about the way things would be. The forward path. The contained life.

There will never be an acceptable answer to the question of why it happened. Before Brett was diagnosed with this freakish pediatric brain tumor—running on the treadmill at the gym one day, falling against the walls in our apartment months later—I was one of those people who believed that "things happen for a reason." Now I know the truth: this just isn't so. There was no rationale for why a healthy young man slipped behind the veil of life. It happened.

But why everything at once? Newborn twins and a death sentence all on the same day?

The question of *why* is like an underexposed negative. The image is so dark that the gray scale is hidden. I studied photography when Brett was very ill and my world lacked definition. What I discovered in the darkroom is that time and light are elemental to exposing the crisp details and sharp tones, to filling the frame and transcending it. Seeing takes time. We have to be patient to draw clarity from the fog.

It's only now that I begin to understand the fluid line existing between past and present, remembrance and breathing, the scent of yesterday and the air of today. Brett has been gone nine years and still I see him in the light of day. It took all that time to reach this place of quiet dwelling, where the surety of the Rocky Mountains, and a new husband and family, meet my gaze each morning and steady me. A husband who lost a wife, boys who lost a mother but who want badly, in their own ways, to feel a family again. *Both Sides Now* is my exploration of holding life and death in the same moment, when overnight you acquire the same life experience as a grandparent but you are still young enough to have children in diapers and the chance for a different future. The question of *why* ultimately becomes *what next* because in order to live and love again you must determine where to place yourself in this altered world.

In the words of Joni Mitchell, *Well something's lost but something's gained.* But first, the story.

PART ONE

Here Is Life

Hope

THE ONLY PROOF OF CURE IS LIFE.

With these words I trusted that the future rested on today. Now you were here. Now you were well. Now we wanted children.

We took the first appointment we could get. It was August 16, 1999. You arrived by taxi. At that time of day, mid-afternoon, it was easy to flag a cab outside your office at Time Inc. at Fiftieth Street and Sixth Avenue. I preferred the anonymity of the subway, only two short blocks from our apartment. Bottled water and *The New Yorker* in hand, I sequestered myself on the downtown No. 1 train, riding four stops to West Seventy-second Street, where I transferred to the crosstown M72 bus. Eleven streets later and through the pretty stretch of Central Park overlooking Strawberry Fields, I exited on the east side, at York Avenue. From here, the hospital was only a four-block walk. The waiting for the trains and buses, meandering on foot and intercepting taxis, it was a way of life. Back then, there was a rhythm to it all.

We'd waited weeks to see Dr. Davis at the Center for Reproductive Medicine and Infertility, and now we sat in his windowed office politely eyeing each other. Dr. Davis was studying you, smiling at me. *Why are we here?* I remember thinking. We're not infertile.

But we did have a problem—not genetics or age or miscarriages—but cancer. Remnants of cancer, I should say, because certainly all traces of the tumor that had lodged in your brain two years ago were now gone. *Why else would we be here?* We knew before your chemotherapy treatment began that it would make you infertile so we banked your sperm. Now, the decision to withdraw your frozen sperm, thaw and mix them with my genetically activated eggs, and then implant the result into an overly stimulated me, was just another way to life unfolding organically. The way it was meant to.

Dressed in a starched white shirt and blue paisley tie, with your summer blazer resting on the back of the chair, you concentrated hard. You were resolved.

Dr. Davis plotted a variety of scientific scenarios, gesturing with his hands to engage us before jotting notes on a small white pad. You reached for my sweaty hand. Every pore in my body resisted being here, but I wanted badly to be a mother, and in vitro fertilization was our only shot. You saw the unease in my eyes and gripped my hand tighter. I watched your slender fingers caress mine, and then looked at you, trying to protect me, while bearing down on all that Dr. Davis was saying. I loved you so fully in that moment. I would do this for you, for us.

But first I had to stuff my sadness over the past, not the grief of yesterday but the way your cancer would etch out a different course for us today and maybe in the future, too. I told myself that it was little more than a mind-set, this business of baby making that Dr. Davis was describing. Like building a model plane: first you identify the parts, then you follow the step-by-step directions; you glue and mold and wait for those pieces to dry before adding accessories; and finally, you've hatched a baby plane, ready to fly.

"There are no guarantees," Dr. Davis told us. "But I think your chances of conceiving are good."

Hope.

In the Beginning We Made an Album Together

BRIDGEPORT, CONNECTICUT, 1979. Your thick hair sways over your body each time you strike the drums. I am in the ninth grade and you are a sophomore at Roger Ludlowe High School in Fairfield. We're at B'nai Israel's Federation of Temple Youth, our temple youth group. We called it BIFTY. We're here to celebrate Jewish music and life, which is code for socializing. I sing in the choir, admiring from a distance the way your skin glows a shade of bronze and lights your eyes like emerald sea glass. You are the tallest person in BIFTY.

Later, we record a folk rock album titled *Creation*, which Cantor Gilbert is proud to produce. He has known us since we were eight years old and in Hebrew school. Look at us now, already past our Bar and Bat Mitzvahs.

Everyone flirts at BIFTY. These are awkward years for me— I am pudgy with a face full of freckles and a thick coat of raspberry blush. I tell my mother more than once, "Brett Zickerman is cute." What she doesn't know—nor do you—is the way I pucker my lips in my bedroom mirror at night, standing two inches from the glass to see what it might look like to kiss and be kissed.

You pay me no attention!

Had I more confidence in myself, I might try harder to make an impression. We never manage a single conversation. Living in Easton is a disadvantage; the town feels like Fairfield's neglected stepchild.

We have no town center, no shopping mall, no beach, no high school of our own. I don't yet appreciate Easton's rural beauty.

My parents insisted I join BIFTY because I am unhappy socially and have just started a new school, where I know nobody. Religion never enters the equation since, like you and your family, we are twice-yearly Jews. We dress up for Rosh Hashanah services, and then again for Yom Kippur. From where I sit in the back of the sanctuary, the focus is on fashion, not God. I am shy when I see you. We never say hello.

Beyond your good looks, there was an appealing easiness about you. You smiled and joked a lot, and were relaxed in your physicality. You were one of those rare people for whom life seemed effortless.

All of the girls in BIFTY wanted to be your girlfriend.

I Was the Girl Who Played Anne Frank

YOU AND YOUR FAMILY CAME TO SEE ME WHEN
I had the lead role in the temple's production of *The Diary of Anne Frank*.
I was a junior in high school and you were a senior, one step closer to
college. These were the years I wanted only to be an actress. The cantor
directed the production. We never spoke after the performance.

You laugh so hard sharing stories about the University of
Maryland and the crazy tailgates at Terps games that you snort and
cry at the same time. You bend forward with your head bowed in a
fit of silliness telling me about the time you and *your boys* borrowed
a dolly from the Coke delivery man, hopped aboard, and then raced
it downhill, collecting beers from the tailgate crowd along the route.
The impact of the dolly hitting the curb hurled the four of you into
the woods, and everyone resurfaced muddy with sticks in their hair.
The crowd went bananas, which made you want to perform the stunt
all over again. There were similar stories about fanatical Terps fans
ripping a goalpost from the field after a winning game and then
carrying it in celebration to the 'Vous Bar, where everyone got drunk
on cheap beer and danced on tables. Your college years were the
best of your life so far, I could tell. And yet at Maryland you discovered your knack for business. You majored in economics and, for

the first time, cared about your GPA and began to have aspirations for the future.

Years after your death, I gather thoughts from your closest college friend, George. He tells me a story of pure friendship. Freshman year a group of you play intramural flag football and everyone calls you *crazy legs* because you are all legs on the field. The team wins the championship game and there is a banquet dinner, at which the school gives each of you a silver turtle charm inspired by Testudo, the university mascot. When we buried you in 2004, George brought his charm. Standing over your grave, he said a private prayer, kissed the charm, and tossed it onto the casket and earth. "From the way he ran, he deserved two charms."

I travel 858 miles away from home, to Northwestern University in Evanston, Illinois. I enroll as a theater major but by the end of my first year have already begun to shy away from wanting to be onstage. Whatever acting passions I felt in high school give way to other interests, like Faulkner, and women's studies and anthropology. My world opens up at Northwestern, and not just because I fall wildly in love with a Muslim the beginning of my junior year. I've grown into my looks; I wear less makeup and go to large parties and feel welcome.

Love and diverse study and friends of all backgrounds puncture my traditional and sheltered upbringing. All through college I work at jobs including waitress and fitness trainer. I learn two enduring lessons: I am a terrible waitress, and health clubs hold promise.

I make friends for life.

We don't re-meet until 1991. You don't remember my name, but you remember that I was the girl who played Anne Frank.

Serendipity at a Hoboken Gym

THURSDAY, SEPTEMBER 5, 1991. I am twenty-five years old living in Hoboken, New Jersey, with Joanie Petrucelli, my oldest childhood friend from Easton. Joanie and I moved to Hoboken for two reasons: to escape the noise of New York City, where we work, and to graduate to a larger space—a two-bedroom, two-bathroom apartment for only slightly more money. Hoboken suits us; it's a small city full of exposed brick, flavorful pizza, thick Italian subs, and views of Manhattan.

Both of us commute during the weekdays; Joanie is in a management training program for Chase Bank, and I work for Ketchum Public Relations. I work with smart people who went to better colleges than I did. Innocence ends as I bank unusual experiences. Like having a top entertainment executive, a client of the firm, hurl expletives over the phone; the best is "Go piss on your leg." Is that even possible? I wonder. The curmudgeon was peeved about what an article in *The New York Times* did not include (never mind that the *Times* covered the story at all). Later, I escort Steven Spielberg's E.T., whom we dub an ambassador for peace, to the World Summit for Children at the United Nations, and to Fort Campbell in Kentucky to headline a benefit concert for children whose parents are deployed in Operation Desert Storm. I get carried away by my own hyperbole over E.T.'s benevolent impact and decide that I want more of this feel-good work. The seed for purposeful work has been planted—it leads me to UNICEF—but first I have to help the *Sports Illustrated* swimsuit model Ashley Montana marry a six-foot hot dog as part of a mock wedding for the opening of Boogie's Diner New York. The concept of selling trendy, expensive jeans and rhinestone T-shirts along with burgers and milk shakes is a novel one, so we stage a marriage of Food and Fashion. Anything is possible when you are young and living in New York City.

But that Thursday in 1991, at 7:00 p.m., I am not negotiating a client crisis, pulling off stunts, badgering the press, or traveling. I am at a Hoboken health club, seated at the bicep machine, rocking back and forth, bored, casing the gym. The place is nearly empty, so it's easy to spot you standing by the wall of mirrors. You are wearing red gym shorts, and I can see that your legs are still tan from summer. You put your hands on your hips, looking around. We recognize each other at the same time.

You wave and walk toward me. I finger-lift my bangs and rise to my feet, ruing my decision to wear a baggy T-shirt.

"Aren't you from Fairfield?" you ask.

"Easton. You're Brett, right?"

"What's your name again?"

From the tentative way you scan the equipment, I'm not surprised to learn that it's your first time here. We talk about BIFTY and Cantor Gilbert, your sister, and our jobs. You have just moved to Hoboken and live with three friends. I've been here a full year already and am a regular at the gym. We talk back and forth for nearly ten minutes, until it becomes clear that I should resume my workout and you should begin yours. The tone shifts. "You look great," you say, leaning forward with your right hand against the bicep machine. You stand a foot from my face, the closest I've ever been to you, those dancing green eyes of yours illuminating your olive skin. My body temperature rises fast. I notice that your forehead starts to sweat.

"Would you like to go out sometime?" you ask.

"Sure," I say immediately.

You commit my home phone number to memory (neither one of us owns a cell phone) and tell me that you'll be in touch. Soon.

I leave the gym at once to phone my mother.

You call an hour later, asking me out for Saturday evening. The next morning you call again to ask if I'd like to see a Broadway play.

It All Felt Right

BEFORE YOU I DATED SOME REAL JERKS — A BRASH, big-lipped dentist from New Jersey, a brooding Polish fencer, and a sweet-talking French waiter with glossy hair. You are the first respectable guy since my college boyfriend, who crushed me two years prior when he reunited with his high school sweetheart (now wife).

From the beginning you win me over with your clear intentions. You call when you say you'll call. You say nice things. You set and keep regular dates. And you tell me two weeks into our relationship that you want to date me exclusively. Our hometown roots put us on a fast track; from the start there is subtle pressure to go forward. Our parents, grandparents, and friends are bursting with questions and expectation. And in a more unspoken way, we feel this, too, the shared dream.

I love the easiness of our relationship, and how relaxed I am with you. There is no need to analyze our status or what we mean to each other. Never once do I question the way you care, never once do I doubt you. We are sure about each other. Before you even utter the words, I read your mind: *I want to marry her.* Somehow it seems ordained that we be together. And this is what I told Joanie and my mom the first time you called me: "I just met the man I'm going to marry."

Five Flights of Stairs

WHAT DOES IT MATTER THAT OUR FIRST APARTMENT is a fifth-floor walk-up? The building sits on pretty, tree-lined West Eighty-seventh Street, steps from Central Park. We have our own patch of concrete. You are twenty-eight; I'm twenty-six. We are healthy and ecstatic to be living in Manhattan.

On weekends I bake apple pie in our miniature kitchen, with its half-size refrigerator and stove. We have no counter space, so I roll dough on the kitchen table. Every time we use the oven we need to open the front door because the ventilation is so poor the smoke alarm sounds. We have a fireplace, too, which we mostly admire for its black marble mantel. But at least twice you make a real fire and we raise the windows and keep the door ajar for hours. Our bedroom is long and skinny, like two bowling lanes. There is no space to walk around the full-size platform bed, and because you sleep on the window side, you jump over me each morning. "Here I come," you tease, which makes us laugh every time. Often I wake before you but feign sleep to enact this ritual.

We assemble a white melamine box for a closet. Life is simple.

Oysters That Shimmer

WE ARE SMOOTH AS TWO POLISHED STONES IN a riverbed.

On Valentine's Day, we sit at a small round table at One If by Land, Two If by Sea in the West Village, famous for special occasions. The rain outside does nothing to dampen the sweet predictability of the evening. Your cheeks are flushed, there's a hint of moisture on your forehead. In between sips of sauvignon blanc, I smile at you in clumsy silence. Oysters and shrimp cocktail shimmer on the table. You move toward me, your eyes fixed on mine. I smile a wide, stupid grin as you bend down on one crisp suit knee to say, "Nancy, I love you and I want to spend the rest of my life with you." Your voice cracks. "Will you marry me?"

I throw my arms around your neck and we kiss.

People from all corners of the restaurant say congratulations, and then the waiter arrives with glasses of champagne. We are too excited to drink, too happy to eat. We call both sets of parents from the pay phone. You have already asked my father for his permission. Which means half the world knows the news. My parents are visiting my grandparents in West Palm Beach, and the first thing my grandma Myrtie says when I tell her about our engagement is "Well, where have you been?"

Moonlight in June

JUNE 26, 1993. Our wedding is just as we hoped: a summer evening in Connecticut. We marry at the Woodbridge Country Club, where my dad's parents are founding members. My grandfather died when I was in college, but it makes my eighty-five-year-old grandma Casey proud as a grande dame to host this affair. She wears a tailored mauve skirt suit and taps her brown wood cane, holding court, while all 184 guests greet her. "Yes, dear, and how are you, dear?" she says to everyone. My dad, who prefers the preppy, casual comfort of L.L.Bean, looks smart in his black tuxedo. Your father, too, moves at the snappy pace of a proud man. His feet glide; why, he's practically dancing as he walks. He squeezes your mother so tight that she worries he might pop the beading off her navy gown. What is it about a wedding and beads? My veil and gown are beaded, as are my bracelet and dangling clip-on earrings. My mother also wears a beaded dress and earrings the color of freshwater pearls. We all sparkle.

Just two grandparents are missing from the family photo, the grandfather of mine who died years earlier, and my other grandfather, who is too frail to attend. Grandma Myrtie stands alongside Grandma Casey and juts her hip out for effect, an "I knew it" smile on her face. And your grandparents Ben and Nettie, dressed in periwinkle and black, look as fashionable as we've ever seen them. Papa Ben's eyes light like fireflies the whole night.

Cantor Gilbert makes a big deal out of marrying us. He feels a stake in our wedding since he's known our families forever and it was through his temple youth group that we first met. He talks about family and community and Anne Frank and BIFTY and the history between us. Guests nod in acknowledgment; everyone here understands that we are supposed to be together. We stand under the chuppah, repeat the prayers and vows, and when all is said and done, the venue for the appetizers announced, you crush the glass with your foot and flash a winning grin. The hair hanging over your forehead brushes mine as we kiss. You loop one arm through mine as we walk down the aisle to the cheers of our guests.

We smile and joke with our friends and family. You give each of your five groomsmen a sport watch, and they mug for the camera. Later, they pick me up and hoist me sideways while you lie across the laps of my five bridesmaids. We're all laughing even though the girls question why I chose magenta organza for their dresses. I don't even like magenta, but it looked good with the flower arrangements. Your Maryland friends are so giddy they punch the air. "Woo, woo, woo," they holler. We are lifted high on chairs while everyone dances in a circle around us.

When I recall our wedding, a more solitary image frames the evening. You and I walk on the golf course, the sun has set, and our photographer captures us in mid-stride. Your tuxedo shirt glistens in the moonlight, as does the long train of my gown. You hold my hand and pull me ever so slightly forward. Your face is cast downward as you concentrate on the steps. For both of us. My head is high as a gentle wind lifts my veil.

Christmas at the Zickermans'

HAVING OUR FAMILIES TEN MINUTES APART IN Connecticut is a balancing act. Equal time for all is what we try to do on weekend visits and the holidays. Thanksgiving with my family one year, your family the next.

But that first year of our married lives we claim our own tradition: Christmas at the Zickermans'. Still in a one-bedroom, we now have a larger space to entertain. Christmas at the Zickermans' brings both families together, including our grandparents. We smell the cold on their faces as they come in the door, throwing coats on our bed, walking about the apartment while rubbing their hands for warmth, commenting on how nice everything looks (it's true that we scrubbed the apartment until it shone). Tea candles glimmer on the glass coffee table and windowsills, and the festive soundtrack to *A Charlie Brown Christmas* plays.

Your job is bartender. On a small patch of kitchen counter, you set up a bar with red wine, seltzer water, soda, and Jim Beam bourbon for your dad. You lay a dark kitchen towel across the counter. You stack highball and wine glasses, and fill the silver ice bucket (a wedding gift). You line the bottles alongside the towel.

The food, however, is the star attraction. These are the years when I scour recipes for days, poring over my cookbooks, current and back issues of *Gourmet* and *Food & Wine*. The more complicated the recipe the better. You encourage my cooking, and take pride in the fact that I rarely make the same dish twice. I can still picture the way you patted your stomach after a pleasing meal, feeling loved and cared for.

That Christmas we have my mother's roasted eggplant red pepper dip; toasted mushroom rolls with cremini, shiitake, and portobello filling; and an assorted vegetable, olive, and cheese plate. I recruit your sister to help make blue cheese and caramelized onion tarts. God knows why we double the recipe for only eleven of us, but somehow we wind up rolling enough pastry dough for eighty-four tarts. We cry over six cups of onions, laughing and commiserating about our excess.

Work and More Work

TIME PASSES QUICKLY. I had landed at UNICEF USA as the manager of media relations. A few years later, when I'm twenty-six, I become director of public relations, creating a small department in the process. The work is exciting and substantial. I comb the newspaper on the morning subway ride, looking for clues as to what emergencies might await me that day. A new turn in the Yugoslav wars? Famine in Iraq? Malaria in Vietnam? I have to be on my game because media call and want to know our response. We have a more difficult time seeding awareness about all the silent crises in developing countries, the way children lack for clean water, basic nutrition, and the right to go to school. Once I meet a small child in El Salvador, a curly-haired girl named Reina, who wears a ripped yellow dress. She ought to be in school, and yet she's sitting in the dirt with hollowed eyes. She's hungry. And why is she alone? I wish that I could take her home with me, but she is just one of millions of children who go hungry in the world. Reina sobers me and is a good counterpoint to the stress I feel trying to manage this job. I could work seven days a week and still it would be insufficient. Because how do you turn your computer off and say, "I've done enough," when it costs just ten cents to save a child from diarrheal dehydration? Or when children lose limbs to land mines and their entire families—mothers, fathers, grandparents, siblings—are killed before their eyes? I see the world as never before with UNICEF.

One December, I spend a humbling afternoon with Audrey Hepburn at the Plaza Hotel in New York City. I had never met her even though she'd been a goodwill ambassador for UNICEF long before I joined the organization. She and her companion, Robert Wolders, had just returned from Somalia. She called it "apocalyptic," like "walking into a nightmare." We were supposed to travel together to Washington, D.C., so that they could appear on *Larry King Live*. But she wasn't feeling well. She didn't know what was wrong; she was tired and her stomach hurt. Still, she consented to one interview in New York since it coincided with an event where she was being honored. At her request, I came early and the three of us sat on a couch in her sitting area. What on earth did we say? She asked me questions about my life. My marriage. My experiences at UNICEF. I'm told she exuded the same graciousness to every staffer. In a matter of days she would learn she had advanced appendiceal cancer. That day, however, she held her stomach, trying to ignore her pain. "Would you like to see my dress for tonight?" Her friend Givenchy had sent it from Paris. She led me by the hand to another room in this sprawling suite where an emerald green gown adorned the bed. She wanted to know if I'd like to try it on.

The news about her cancer comes quickly, and I wonder how she acted with such dignity and peace of spirit when surely she must have been afraid.

Early in our marriage we have dinner with friends on the Upper West Side who have a black cat called Sneakers. He has white feet and a white chin, and our friends think he resembles Abraham Lincoln. I am petrified of cats. I must have been a mouse in a prior life. While we are dining on asparagus goat cheese lasagna with béchamel sauce, Sneakers escapes from his dungeon and bounds into the living room. "The cat, get the cat," I shout, lifting my legs onto the glass dining table. At once you jump up, help catch Sneakers, and return him to the bedroom, this time with kitchen twine tied from the bedroom to the bathroom door.

My phobias were transparent. Like when we took a catamaran in St. Martin and you maneuvered the sail and boom, gripping the tiller while I crouched with my tush raised high so that a shark wouldn't bite me. You never teased me, you were always so kind. Nothing in the world made you afraid back then, or if you had fears, I never knew of them.

You love your job at Time Warner, which now has you, only thirty, representing the Money and Fortune brands for the company's first Internet portal. You dream about the Pathfinder network, and it's all that you can talk about: how to develop the business, how to grow the individual brands, how to attract advertisers, how to serve as a resource for consumers. You snap your briefcase shut each morning ready to take on the day. There's no time for breakfast, you'll grab something on the run, prospects await. Even your kiss has energy. Few people see the potential for the Internet to transform business the way you do. You're one step ahead, enrolling in New York University's graduate program for media ecology, where you study with the media guru Neil Postman. The day you graduate there is a downpour, but the rain hardly dampens your smile, or your shoes, which you shield with galoshes. Dressed in a purple robe, you stand on the street holding an oversize green Money umbrella. You can't wait to get back to work the next morning.

As time goes by, each of us intent on building a career, we don't always share passion for the other's professional life. I am so immersed in the language of UNICEF—life and death and survival—that it's sometimes strange for me to hear the urgency with which you speak about the Internet. We sit at a bistro with friends and you describe your plans to grow revenue through online ad sales and marketing partnerships. "This is going to be an entirely new way of business," you predict. We raise our glasses of wine to toast your success. But this world of yours is vague for me. I can't see it. When our friends ask me about UNICEF, it's hard for me to stop talking. I know that you are proud of me for caring so much, but sometimes your eyes gloss over when I ramble about the situation in Haiti or how we plan to commemorate the Day of the African Child.

When I leave UNICEF, in 1996, I imagine that we have years ahead of us to lead quieter lives. I tap some of my former public relations contacts and begin consulting from home. *We have plenty of time to map our future because we are still so young.*

It Started with Burping

AT FIRST WE THOUGHT IT WAS FUNNY. You burped and hiccuped repeatedly. You burped while chewing, showering, talking on the phone, at odd and unexpected moments, as if you'd been drinking, which you hardly did at all.

One day we stopped laughing. I don't remember which day it was. The punch line had been revealed too many times. It was clear that you couldn't stop burping, and suddenly there was something immediate about your health.

Neither one of us imagined there was anything really wrong with you since you'd never been sick with anything more serious than a head cold.

When over-the-counter antacids didn't help, you saw your internist. You kept seeing him as you dropped weight and had trouble sleeping. It seemed strange that your physician wasn't able to offer anything to you beyond Prevacid, which was then prescription only. You had a chest X-ray and all was clear. You delayed calling your doctor again even as you grew sicker.

I was relieved when you let me join you at the gastroenterologist's. A specialist would make sense of your discomfort, I was sure. The doctor was a kind, middle-aged man with a Greek accent, but he, too, had trouble making sense of it all after an endoscopy of your esophagus showed nothing remarkable. Were you very stressed? he wondered. I wondered, too. Fear of the unknown, fear of anything seriously wrong began to torment you.

Five months from the time you started to hiccup and burp, your reflux worsened and it made you nauseated, which, on top of your anxiety, further diminished your appetite. You always had a soft spot for sweets, but not even chocolate rugelach cookies tempted you. I stocked the freezer with foods you enjoyed—rocky road ice cream, bagels, and blueberry blintzes. You hated a messy freezer even if you appreciated my efforts.

What once united, now divided. The more you turned away from food, the harder I tried to get you to eat. I fussed over hearty, caloric meals like chicken breasts stuffed with Gorgonzola cheese and rib eye steaks topped with beurre blanc sauce. I bought you shrimp cocktail and whitefish salad. I made mashed potatoes five different ways: with cream, bacon, chives, horseradish, and parsnips. "Thank you for dinner," you'd say, as you moved the food around your plate, leaving it cut and rearranged but uneaten. I cleaned my plate and yours with a manic energy. That you wouldn't, or couldn't, eat felt like an injustice, to both of us. And there were nights when I let my fears slip, making you feel bad as you withdrew further from me and from all that you once desired. We were both struggling with the words, wanting but too afraid to understand. Neither one of us could imagine things getting worse.

I Wondered If You Were Depressed

YOU WERE NEVER THE DEPRESSED TYPE. I was the one genetically prone to swings of emotion, to feeling giddy and confident one day, sunken and overwhelmed the next. But you, Brett, were as stable and happy a person as I'd ever met. These qualities are among the things I loved most about you. You were gentle and unobtrusive, never seizing attention for the sake of doing so—a rarity in a place like New York City, where people have to raise their voices just to be visible.

Do you know that over five hundred people filled the Riverside Memorial Chapel for your funeral on February 24, 2004? They had to open the basement level to fit all the mourners, and the crowd seated downstairs watched the service on small televisions. I've saved the eulogies, poems, cards, and drawings, including one from a colleague that read, "He changed my life because he knew this one secret: you make your own happiness."

Which is why your peculiar withdrawal in the months leading up to your diagnosis unnerved me so much. From me, yes, it hurt when you pulled away, drawing deeper into your interior world. But it was even more disorienting when you lost energy and passion for your job.

Just as your career summited (you were now a vice president), your health waned. Going to work drained you. Shaving, fixing your tie, and getting out the door each morning made you short of breath. And when you returned home after nine-hour days that rapidly grew shorter, your skin looked purple and sweaty. "I'm so tired," you said, kissing me hello and passing out in bed in one continuous sweep of motion.

By December 1997, you'd lost nearly twenty pounds. Your six-foot frame could handle the weight loss, but you looked worn and diminished. I'm still haunted by the brownish black circles that shadowed your eyes. Where was the man I had married four and a half years earlier? The man with the generous inch to hold who loved to eat and laugh over featherbrained films like *Caddyshack* and even sillier television programs starring the British comedy character Mr. Bean. Where was the man with the bronzed, high cheekbones, lush hair, and clear eyes? Where was the man who tapped his hands to the beat of a Springsteen tune the same way he once swayed over his drums? "Please tell me what's going on," I'd ask repeatedly, at first in gentle tones, but later with pitched agitation.

"I don't know, I just need to rest" was how you responded each time, turning away from me as you spoke. You lay down on our pretty comforter with your back to me, and you erected a mighty wall that left me feeling disconnected. I'd sit next to you on the bed reading a book or magazine, perhaps a glass of wine in hand, but it was your company I wanted.

Yes, I thought you were depressed—as though some inexplicable crisis you couldn't articulate was making you sick. Depression had to be responsible, because what else could it be? The doctors found nothing physically wrong with you, and you wouldn't speak. I did not fully understand your terror, the way it paralyzed you and was dividing us.

You had to be depressed because you were only thirty-three, a healthy, successful businessman, an adored son, brother, friend, a fine husband. I was only thirty-one, and we had the whole of our lives ahead of us. Someday we'd have children, and when our children were grown, we'd hold hands like the elderly couples we used to see walking in Riverside Park, wearing light blue cardigans and stretch trousers. Were they headed somewhere? It was hard to say. Time appeared on their side.

I Knew You Weren't Depressed

EARTH TO BRETT, I WANTED TO SHOUT. *Where are you*?

You were in the bathroom, vomiting. You tried to keep it from me at first, creeping there in the middle of the night. You even turned the water on to muffle the sound.

One night, while we were together on the bed, you told me that you felt dizzy when you turned your head to the left. You were lying on your right side, facing me. "What do you mean?" I asked. "How?" It started happening a few days ago, you told me. Stopping there, not elaborating, leaving me to complete the thoughts. Our sheets soft and wrinkled beneath us, your flesh wrapped in them, ghostly.

I still didn't understand the meaning of your illness, but I no more doubted this: depression was not responsible. The next morning in a panic I called your psychologist—the one I made you see to talk about what you were feeling. You wanted to please me, and possibly because you were scared, you were pliant. "Something is very wrong," I told your psychologist, not the least bit concerned about overstepping the client confidentiality code. "We need your help." This would be the first of many times I would sound the alarm for you, advocating for your needs since you could not.

I never met that therapist, but I'm grateful he got you an appointment with a neuro-oncologist at Columbia University two days later. You confided about how frequently you were vomiting, about the sharp, violent tremors in your head, and how you had passed out, briefly, twice during business flights. *Why, Brett, why didn't you tell me? Why didn't you mention this to Uncle Harvey? You stayed with him in California; he might have taken you to see one of his medical colleagues at Stanford. Why aren't you answering me?* From the blank, defeated expression on your face, it was clear that you had no answers, that you hadn't wanted to worry us, that silence was a form of protection.

Life Upended

THE TEN-MINUTE TAXI RIDE FROM OUR WEST SIDE apartment to the hospital felt otherworldly. The trees lining Riverside Park jutted upright like stilts, as though they had no roots to ground them.

Dr. Casilda Balmaceda, the neuro-oncologist, was in her thirties, not much older than we were. Dressed in her white doctor coat and gray trousers, she shook our cold hands and led us into a brown conference room, gently closing the door behind her.

All was quiet.

And then, leveling her gaze at you, she said, "You have a brain tumor."

You said nothing. You put your head down and wept over the table.

Tears and terror and a nausea I could taste came quickly.

"I don't know exactly what kind it is," Dr. Balmaceda said, "but you will need surgery, and soon."

"Will he be all right?" I asked, my hands reaching out to cover yours.

"I don't know," she said. "I'm so sorry."

Relief and the Plastic Brain

YOU WERE SO SICK AND SO TIRED THAT YOU almost welcomed the diagnosis. You were relieved to know that you weren't crazy. We saw the demon tumor ourselves, in vivid contrast, tacked to the white fluorescent board in your surgeon's office. It was the size of a small rodent. A mouse or a dwarf rat.

No sooner did Dr. Balmaceda break the news to us (*life really did combust in that moment*), than she escorted us upstairs to the ninth floor, where your young neurosurgeon-to-be, Dr. Michael Sisti, greeted us in his plush office. He had a kind face, a soft voice, and bright blue eyes.

We stood looking at your brain scans as Dr. Sisti explained that the mass was lodged around the lower part of your cerebellum and down into your left medulla. We had no real knowledge of the inner workings of the human brain, how it is made up of over 100 billion nerve cells capable of 1,000 trillion connections—all happening in a squishy, three-pound lump the size of a cantaloupe.

Neither one of us had ever seen an MRI of the brain before, and here was yours: black, white, and abnormal. What focused our attention was when Dr. Sisti raised the possibility that your tumor could be benign. "You might not need chemotherapy or radiation at all if it's an ependymoma.

"Come sit," he said gently, sensing your physical exhaustion.

I remember how you and I hung on those words: *it could be benign.*
Dr. Sisti made no promises; the actual tumor would need to be
confirmed by a pathology report, after your surgery, which we sched-
uled, with precision and haste, for the following week.

We sat in matching blue armchairs. You kept staring beyond the
good doctor, out the window at the Hudson River. You couldn't follow
the conversation and had a pained look on your face. I was fixated on
a pink, plastic, life-size model of a brain on his large mahogany desk,
half-listening as he told us about all the intricate cases he had operated on and how he would approach yours. Dr. Sisti tried to reassure
us even as he laid out multiple strategies for dealing with tumors in
the posterior fossa, wherever that was. Again, he speculated on how
the large size and location of your tumor were consistent with epen-
dymomas. "But if it's malignant, that's another story."

I started to take notes since the conversation was so surreal.
As clear as *lesion* and *fourth ventricle* and *cranioectomy* and *chemotherapy*
looked on paper, I felt disconnected from them, the pen a foreign
object in my hand. Still, I forced myself to jot down the words since I
would never remember them otherwise.

My foot fell asleep, and as I began to twist it awake, I felt an
odd tension within my body—an airy, untethered rustling. Part of
me wanted to bolt from Dr. Sisti's office, to run from this dark curtain
he was opening. I wanted to escape back in time, to unwritten scripts.
Not youth so much as possibility. *The future with children and a house
with a white fence and you mowing the lawn and grilling on weekends and me
cooking vegetables grown from our garden.* Life had turned for us in this
moment, regardless of the outcome of your surgery.

It might have been naïve and vain to feel this way, that life would
never cut *us* unexpectedly (no one deserves terrible things to happen),
but really, we had been lucky up until now. I stayed in that blue chair
in Dr. Sisti's office because at last there was some explanation for
your declining health, and he appeared genuine and knowledgeable
about how to help you. We spent nearly an hour with him, and at
some point he told us that he was likely the only neurosurgeon from

New Jersey who neither played golf nor liked Bruce Springsteen. "I'll forgive you," you said.

Dr. Sisti weighed the variety of possible tumors and treatment protocols, from good to moderate to bad. "I hope that the treatments have the highest chance of success for this nice couple," he would later write in one of his reports. Under normal circumstances, I'd have drilled down into every perceived scenario. Not this time. I kept looking at the brain on his desk, half-expecting it to run and leap from the window into the Hudson River. Reality was shifting for me in this moment. I couldn't understand why the plastic brain stayed static or the desk hadn't budged. Why did the view of the river remain unobstructed? Why, when the earth had dropped the way it did for us, was nothing moving?

Love and Fear

THAT NIGHT, I COULDN'T STOP CRYING. You brought me peppermint tea and sat beside me on the black couch. "I'm going to be all right," you said, rubbing my back. "Now we know what we're dealing with, and I'll just do everything I need to do to get better."

I believed in you, that you would do anything in your power to heal. But we really didn't know the full extent of your condition yet, or that the tumor was malignant, which meant this wasn't a one-off surgical excision but real brain cancer. Cancer that would put you through a hellish year of treatment. We didn't understand how difficult and humiliating it would be for you to learn to walk again after your surgery, or that the lifetime dose of radiation to the back of your head would fry your surgical scar, causing it to leak spinal fluid, or that your hair would never grow back, or that one of the first chemotherapy agents you were given, a nasty drug called vincristine, would cause permanent neuropathy severe enough that you had to use a cane walking a dozen steps from the kitchen to the bedroom in our small apartment. Months later, you would fall on the street, and as I rushed toward you, to help, you lashed out in a rare moment of anger: "Damn it, Nancy, let me do it on my own."

We had no knowledge of this future when we learned of your diagnosis, the Day of No Going Back. Except for the wind brushing against the tree outside our bedroom window, all was quiet that night. Neither of us felt up to talking. We lay as husband and wife and held each other as we hadn't done in months. The way we were that evening, with our naked fears and love sprawled on the bed, was pure and beautiful, as if time itself was patient.

You Went to Work

YOU WENT BACK TO WORK AT TIME INC. A FEW
months after your surgery. Work was your reprieve and your equal-
izer, and it was where you felt most hopeful because there you had a
sense of purpose apart from your disease.

Your colleagues and bosses kept you abreast of developments not
because they needed your immediate input but because they wanted you
to feel validated. And you kept up, reading the e-mails, returning the
phone calls, piecing everything together as best you could. You exerted
what little energy you had in trying to maintain your business edge.

"How are you, Brett?" your colleagues wanted to know, daily.

"I'm great, just great," you answered.

One day there was a storm. It was bad enough that school was
canceled and yet you insisted on heading to the office. "Brett, this
is crazy. What if you slip and fall?" I said. But you wouldn't hear of
staying home. "I've missed enough work, I'll be fine."

"Please don't go. I'm sure everyone will understand. I just don't think
this is a smart idea. Can you please at least wait until the roads clear?"

"I have to go," you told me, pulling on your trench coat. You
reached for your scarf and gloves and baseball cap from the top shelf
of the closet. Then, your cane.

It was hard to argue with something so normal as going to
work, and you taking the town car, not just in inclement weather

but every day, did comfort me. Sending a car was a magnanimous gesture on your company's part; the subway germs would have killed you, and we couldn't afford taxis two or more times a day to shuttle you from our apartment to your midtown office, to the hospital, and back again. We didn't yet have a car in Manhattan; without this very basic support, I don't know how you would have been able to resume your career.

When you left that morning, I was still in your white undershirt, warm and crinkled from sleep. You hadn't even taken time for breakfast. You kissed me goodbye, and as I closed the door behind you I felt queasy. I walked to the window in our living room and saw the driver standing by the passenger side. He was waiting for you in case you needed help. You acknowledged the driver and lowered yourself into the backseat, resting both hands atop your cane. The driver slammed the door and the car was off.

Watching you leave on that snowy morning filled me with immense sadness. There was a listless quality about the way the snow fell. The sky was unusually dark for this 8:00 a.m. hour, and because I didn't have to be anywhere that day (a perk of having my own business), I wanted only to climb back under the fluffy weight of our down comforter. So I did. Gloom enveloped me there like sweltering air; it was hard to breathe, hard to move. Why was it that just as you were feeling stronger, I felt weaker? I'd been sturdy and positive for months, propping you up, managing well. Even I admired my ability to stay calm in the midst of crisis. And now that the emergencies were behind us, there was only the numbing sensation of trauma and real life. I wanted you home with me because your very presence reassured me. Instead, I lay in bed and stared mindlessly into your cedar closet. You'd left the door open. Your business shirts lined the front pole, and you kept a full jar of spare change on the top shelf.

How I would love to see you again, bald and sweet as a peach, fixing your tie in the bedroom mirror as you gave me a fighting smile.

Eventually, yes, I started my pajama-clad morning from my tiny, makeshift office at the back of our dining room. We'd partitioned the room with long black file cabinets and two of my mother's paintings, which we suspended from the ceiling. I sipped my coffee and began, like always, by looking out the window. Looking outside was easier than facing the Post-it notes taped to my desk. I needed time to root myself, to acclimate to phone calls and office work and the business of the day. In such empty moments I found that I could separate from your cancer. I gazed at the cracked concrete of the building adjacent to ours. Its imperfections soothed me.

You Wore a Hat

NO ONE WELCOMES A CANCER DIAGNOSIS. But some people come to embrace and even own their illnesses. They advocate by wearing pink shirts and yellow wristbands and participating in fund-raising walks. Not you. Ever. I sometimes wanted to go to cancer support groups and connect with other brain tumor patients and their families. Living in New York City, we had ample opportunities, but in the early years we kept to ourselves.

Counseling gave me an outlet, and for you, balancing work and your intensive treatment schedule was enough. You went for full brain and spine radiation every day for six weeks, where you wore a carbon mask and slid into a cradle that immobilized your head and neck, while shielding the rest of your body from the toxic rays. They blasted you with 3,600 shots of radiation to your spine and another 5,400 units to your skull, enough to stunt growth and cause learning difficulties in children.

When you finished this regimen, you were nauseated and exhausted, but time was ticking so Dr. Balmaceda started you right away on chemotherapy with three powerful drugs. There were no known protocols for medulloblastomas in adults, so she conferred with specialists around the country to create the best plan of action for you. How strangely lucky, I always thought, that Uncle Harvey was a pediatric oncologist. As chief of staff of Lucile Packard Children's

Hospital and chair of pediatrics at Stanford University's School of Medicine, he either knew or could quickly reach all the top cancer doctors in the country. We didn't make a move without him.

Brain cancer is impossible to hide. You had a two-inch scar on the back of your head, you were bald and without eyelashes, and much as you loathed to admit it, you needed your cane. "Look at me," you said one night in front of the bathroom mirror. I kissed your forehead and assured you that I loved you just the same. Yet you didn't feel loving toward yourself, which was another loss to accept. You never left home without a cap. The hats became your armor, and they gave you strength.

We buried you in your navy blue Olympics cap, the one given to you by my friend Gwen, a cancer survivor. She bought it at the 2002 Winter Olympic Games in Salt Lake City.

How was it that the incision on the back of your head leaked small traces of spinal fluid, but it was my scars that felt raw and exposed? I felt a tightness across my mouth, as if my lips were sewn together, and my eyes twitched and winced without warning. Everywhere I went, kind people commented. "You look tired. You look sad." Fear was always bobbing in my head, particularly at night, when the recurrent image of a noose around my neck would startle me awake.

I wish that I hadn't felt so suffocated by your disease. That I might have kept my confidence during that first long year. Rarely, you allowed yourself to think, *What if I'm not cured?*

Time changes the vantage point from which we view existence. Back then, in the midst of your treatment, it concerned me that you and your parents might be in denial. All of you were quick to look past the bad days, when your body hurt and felt feverish and you were too tired and sick to eat or make small talk. I got rattled over losing my glass of water in the apartment, but you resisted everyday nuisances. You focused on the future, on one goal only: a total cure. It's what we all wanted.

There were many moments I wanted to shout, "Don't you get it? This is serious!" *Why is no one but me noticing how the oven door slams louder than it used to? And how the laundry smells dirty even when it's clean, and the water from the bathroom faucet looks yellow, and the air is so heavy around us.*

With the exception of hurting someone you love, there is no right or wrong way to cope with a life-threatening illness. I came to see that you were right to feel the way you did. We go where we need to go. For your own survival you had to leap ahead, to a place beyond the internment of your cancer, where you could live and dream like a healthy man. Was this a form of denial? Perhaps it's what Susan Sontag meant in *Illness as Metaphor* when she wrote:

Illness is the night-side of life, a more onerous citizenship. Everyone who is born holds dual citizenship, in the kingdom of the well and in the kingdom of the sick. Although we all prefer to use only the good passport, sooner or later each of us is obliged, at least for a spell, to identify ourselves as citizens of that other place.

Ours was an uncomfortable reality. For you, and for me.

One Day I Bought a Perfume Called Happy

YOU REMAINED SO POSITIVE THAT I WAS CERTAIN your attitude was making you well. Twelve months of radiation and chemotherapy, and all signs of your cancer were gone. The original tumor had been removed and no other lesions or cancer cells showed on your brain scans. You were feeling triumphant, as though you had conquered Mount Everest.

I went to Macy's and bought a perfume called Happy by Clinique. I liked the clean scent and hoped the name would bring good luck. Every morning I spritzed Happy on my wrists and neck and thought pleasing thoughts. "Let's make it a good day," I'd say to myself. A small forward-moving gesture.

"I told you I'm going to be all right," you said, hugging me when you returned home from the office at night, the way you used to. I dug my fingers into the back of your neck, clamping down hard until you said, "Ouch," and we laughed.

With no more treatment in sight, and cancer no longer a daily menace, I started volunteering for Dress for Success, an organization that helps low-income women move from welfare to work, and also picked up a few paying public relations clients. You spent full days at the office and resumed traveling. I dusted off my cookbooks and foodie magazines and made lavish meals. You craved my garlic clam pizza from *Food & Wine*. We'd been married only a month when I first stumbled upon it. The dough was always a bit misshaped, but the cornmeal crust was sturdy and crisp.

We saw movies and friends, went out to dinner on the Lower East Side, and visited our families in Connecticut. I enrolled in a black-and-white photography class. My heart swelled each time I saw an image appear from the shadows of the paper. And you played nine holes of golf with your college friends that fall. You were a little wobbly on your feet, but you took it in stride. You and "your boys" even smoked cigars.

We bought an apartment, too, in the same building on West 104th Street where we had been subletting. I squealed when I saw the listing in *The New York Times* because we were already approved by the cooperative's board of directors and living only one floor below the tenants who wished to sell. I thought it was a great omen. The new apartment was spacious. I had an office with a door and there was a spare bedroom to fill, we hoped soon, with a child. We enlisted my brother, Greg, an architect in Manhattan, to redesign the master bathroom with a stand-up glass shower and bench. It was your idea, and when the project was complete, you gave tours to all our neighbors. We also took a small room, formerly a maid's quarters, and enlarged it into an open kitchen with an island countertop. It was our first real home, and we felt proud to make it ours, blending the old, prewar features with modern elements, renovating for the future.

And we traveled again, to visit my college roommate Julie and her husband, Rick, in Colorado. They hadn't seen you since your diagnosis, so this was a real celebration, to come together as in better days, enjoying the mountain air and eating Vietnamese food in downtown Denver. The white house with the picket fence we'd once coveted across the street from Cranmer Park was still occupied, but maybe one day it would be ours, you said. I smiled at the very notion. Sometime after this trip, we even went to London. We'd never been there, so we booked a trip, and the next week, or so it seemed, we were staring at the Crown Jewels. We spent more time walking and going out—from morning until night—than we had in the previous two years combined. The London trip was a turning point for us. It was such a rush to feel alive again.

We Made a Choice

YOU NEVER ASKED ME IF I WAS READY TO HAVE children. But in the aftermath of your treatment and the sweet eighteen months that followed, you let me come to the decision myself, to be able to trust in that sort of complete future again. You were ready, and I saw your face soften and light when you held the newborn babies of our friends and cousins. You rocked and walked and fed them as if they were your own.

The world was full of infants. Soon, it was all we could talk about. Parenthood gave us a focus and a goal.

Life really had returned to the new normal for us. We continued to feel fulfilled by our work; we had dates; and at least once a week I asked you to please pick up your pile of clothes beside the bed. In 1999, the world was reeling from the Columbine school massacre, where two students killed twelve others and a teacher before committing suicide. John F. Kennedy, Jr., and his pretty bride died in a plane crash, and NATO bombed Yugoslavia for its barbaric human rights abuses. Everywhere, the media were buzzing about Y2K and the millennium. Life was happening all around us. It seemed essential to move away from the private fears that had foreshortened our vision, to pay attention to the world, to care and want to be part of it.

Every three months you went for a routine scan, an MRI, which continued to show no signs of disease. With each successive test behind you, we emigrated toward life. Meditating to Springsteen's "Land of Hope and Dreams" helped, too:

Well, tomorrow there'll be sunshine and all this darkness past.

Time passed like this, both of us going about our lives, healing on our own, dreaming together. You were feeling so good, that in our minds, you became cured. It was subtle at first, the signs evident by the fullness of your days. *We made you cured.* None of the doctors used such language, but I wouldn't remember this. The precise wording was that you were being treated with "curative intent"—quite a different reality than pronouncing you cancer-free. It all blurred for me, for us. My own desire, and yours, and your heavenly run of renewed health, allowed us to leap from wellness to cure. Against this backdrop, it's no wonder that the narrative soon became "He is cured."

The only proof of cure is life. It was Uncle Harvey who spoke the words while at your parents' house for Thanksgiving. We were just beginning to think about starting a family. Life is the only antidote to death, he was saying. Seven simple words and a new philosophy for living. Here was certainty we could grasp.

Time would reveal this simple wisdom to us again and again, not then, but later, when your cancer came back and your odds of survival dimmed. "You are not a statistic," your second neuro-oncologist told you after delivering especially bad news. "There is either all of you or none of you."

We chose life. We made a choice to have children. It was the most hopeful thing we could do, to live as though you were cured. We talked about probability, about the likelihood of you or me getting hit by a reckless taxi driver or stepping off the curb into the metal of a city bus. It could happen.

There was no real way to know if your cancer would ever return. At least among children with medulloblastomas, many never have a recurrence. So it was possible, yes. *The only proof of cure is life.*

I Made You Ring Bells

NOVEMBER 1999, I WAS NERVOUS AND DILIGENT, reading all the in vitro fertilization literature, talking to women friends who had successfully been through it, chatting up the nurses each morning when required to do blood work, and engaging in faux friendships with other mothers-in-waiting in the reception area. Cornell's Center for Reproductive Medicine was a baby mill: the women rushed in each morning as soon as the doors opened at 7:00. (If you arrived even fifteen minutes later, chances were good you'd be without a seat.) They dressed in velour sweat suits. They desperately wanted babies. Eyes fixed on anyone with a swollen belly.

My eggs were fine, your frozen sperm had enough potential to be life-giving, and our lives were back on track. I detached myself from the stories overheard in the waiting room, hushed conversations that revealed the angst, heartbreak, and determination of women of varying ages now in their third or fourth cycles. Their talk should have made me nervous; there were no guarantees in this costly process. Instead, I thought, *That won't be me. We don't have fertility problems.*

I gained a healthy five pounds and responded well to the cocktail of hormones I was injecting into my body. We trusted science to get me pregnant, with Lupron, Gonal-f, and progesterone shots.

I got pregnant right away. But it wouldn't last. The nurse called to say, "You're pregnant, although..." My numbers were too low to sustain a pregnancy. Heat in the back of my throat exploded into tears. "We'll try again," you said. I knew that the news disappointed you, too, even if you tried to be positive, reminding me that I had indeed gotten pregnant. It never entered my mind that I could be half-pregnant and then have a miscarriage. My faith shaken, my trust eroded, I might have bludgeoned your cancer were it still alive.

We waited several months before trying again. Our neighbor and psychologist minister friend, Erik Kolbell, recommended that we treat this next cycle with "cautious optimism." So I changed my stance. This time I was guarded and kept to myself. I sat in the waiting room and read the newspaper or a book, avoiding conversation with the other ladies-in-waiting. When my name was called, I walked quietly to the station where my blood was drawn. We held back from broadcasting every step to cousins and friends, telling only immediate family members. On the eve of my egg retrieval I botched the injection of HCG (human chorionic gonadotropin) at 1:30 a.m., mixing it with water instead of medicine. Without a boost of HCG, the hormone to stimulate ovulation, there can be no viable pregnancy. The shot had to be given at a specific time in order to stagger the next day's retrievals. "I can do it," I reassured you. "I don't want you waking up in the middle of the night." And yet I must have been groggy from sleep or in a dream state; there is no other explanation for how I could have fumbled such a crucial step.

When the same nurse as for my first pregnancy called the next morning to ask what had happened (I had already gone for blood work), my body caved because I sensed disaster. "No," I cried. "There must be something you can do!"

Forced to end this second cycle, I crumbled. Erik came over that night; we ordered pizza and split a bottle of wine. You sat with your arm around my shoulder, feeling equally despondent but trying to comfort me. I was sobbing hard, raging at God. "Why are all these bad things happening? What kind of black cloud is over us?" I asked Erik. "Why is nothing easy?" The questions would haunt me for years.

What I wanted was to turn our fate around. My faith may have been teetering, but I still believed in God or a higher being (they were indistinguishable to me). Even though the life we'd once imagined had deceived us, I was convinced that something bigger than me, larger than us—some Higher Grace—could blanket and heal us. Blind faith also made me less alone in my worry; I was able to question and doubt God without casting blame.

You wanted no part of my spiritual quest, your capacity for faith, limited as it was before your illness, shattered. But you were a good sport. At the same time I was actively channeling God, I wrote affirmations on pink Post-its and placed them all over the apartment. "I trust in the order of nature and in my body's ability to conceive through in vitro. I am capable, deserving, and it is entirely possible for me to conceive, carry to full term, and deliver a healthy baby without fear." They were the first reminders I saw when I brushed my teeth in the morning and while reaching for a coffee mug over breakfast.

In the middle of our third in vitro cycle, I bought several books on feng shui and decided to have a spiritual cleansing march. Our contractor's wife led the procession. She made you walk from room to room ringing a bell. "This is really weird," you kept mumbling, just loud enough for me to hear. At first I shushed you. "Please, just do this." But even I couldn't keep a straight face when she began to sway her arms as if in a trance. You staggered against the wall when we rounded the corner to the bedroom, and that made us snicker. We tried to suppress it, but our giggles kept spilling over, like foam sliding off a root beer float. Still, I believed that feng shui could vaporize the past, bringing to the surface all our wishes for a healthful future.

You weren't about to buy into this walk of faith—you thought feng shui was ridiculous—but at least you honored my intentions. Like prayer, anything unseen or inexplicable, anything not logical was challenging for you. What was the harm, I suggested, in trying a new approach? "Keep an open mind."

Wishing It Until I Believed It

PRACTICING FENG SHUI WITH FEVERISH INTENTION
kept me focused on staying positive. By October 2000, I was as
humbled as I'd ever been—your cancer diagnosis and two failed
fertility attempts over the past twelve months had made sure of that.
I really don't know if it was faith or hope, or both, but my heart
was pure like a newborn's each time I said my mantra. "I trust in the
order of nature and in my body's ability to conceive through in vitro.
I am capable, deserving, and it is entirely possible for me to conceive,
carry to full term, and deliver a healthy baby without fear."

The more often I said this mantra, the calmer I felt about our
prospects. Fear of IVF not working still made my body freeze, but a
few tight hand squeezes released enough blood flow to center me
again. I wasn't afraid of your cancer returning then. I only wanted
to get pregnant.

I felt unusually quiet inside as the date of the next egg retrieval
neared. I'd responded well to all the hormone-inducing drugs. I ate
healthily, took walks, meditated, and went to acupuncture at the
recommendation of a friend who swore it had primed her body for
conception (she had twins). You and I had a tacit pact that we would
not talk about this either. No dark thoughts. I just had a feeling, a
premonition I could taste like sweat on my tongue, that I would get
pregnant. I wished it until I believed it.

The egg retrieval was a fifteen-minute procedure to suction follicles from my ovaries; those follicles with the healthiest eggs would
then be placed in an incubator so the eggs could be mated with your
sperm. The clinic did hundreds of routine retrievals each month.
Which is why we must have skimmed the fine print when signing the
consent forms.

In all, the doctor extracted eleven eggs, a respectable number
to work with and the highest number I'd produced yet. Within a few
days, and certainly by the time of the embryo transfer, three days
later, we'd know which of the eleven eggs would survive, which
would die off, and which would be of high enough quality to fertilize
and implant.

I tried not to think about the castaways.

Mom took the Metro North train from Connecticut to join us
since you were moving offices that day and the hospital required an
escort. We assumed we'd be home by mid-morning, in time for her to
catch an afternoon train. You planned to leave work early, meet me
back at the apartment, and order Vietnamese food for dinner.

For the first half hour after the retrieval, I lay in a recovery room
with ten other women, all of whom had had their retrievals, too. They
looked fine and one by one began to dress and leave the hospital. It
hurt to straighten my body, so I curled up in a fetal position. "Don't
worry," the nurses explained. "It's normal to feel tightness and mild
pain, it won't last."

Mom thought I should rest at home. "Wait ten minutes," I told
her. Which turned into another ten minutes, then an hour, and then
another. Somewhere I lost count, because each time she asked if I
was ready to leave, it was harder to sit up. It wasn't until early afternoon, long after my fellow retrievers had left, when I felt clobbered
by nausea and clenching pain moving higher up my body, that it
occurred to the medical staff that something was wrong.

They took me in for a sonogram. Blood filled the tiny screen
in a swirl of black, my anxiety now rivering a fresh current of pain
that had me moaning. "Typically the bleeding stops on its own,"

the staff explained. "Try to take deep breaths."

Mom called you at the office to say I was having complications. By the time you arrived, some blood vessels had ruptured. "It feels like someone is stabbing me," I moaned. I had never felt pain of this sort. Every time I took a breath it felt like I was choking. At last the staff realized that my case was not *typical*. They paged the doctor (he'd come once before) and took a fresh look at the sonogram. I was bleeding into my abdomen. Quickly they increased the morphine and pumped some sort of antianxiety drug through the same IV. The hemorrhaging would not stop. The doctor looked grave as he explained that he would need to do an emergency laparoscopy, make an incision in my pelvis, to cauterize the bleeding.

You were as scared as I was: I saw fear in the tightness of your jawbone and the steel green of your eyes. Life had reversed itself. Now I was the patient and you were the concerned spouse. Bleeding of this sort hadn't happened here in fifteen years; it was extremely rare for an egg retrieval patient to hemorrhage that extensively.

In the chaos of the moment, there was no time to think about the future. "Worst case scenario," the doctor said, pulling on his gloves, "is that we'll have to take your ovaries."

You and Mom kissed my forehead, propping your arms around each other as they wheeled me off to surgery.

When I woke, the doctor told us he'd removed several large blood clots from my ovaries, abdomen, and pelvic area. The clots were triggered by my hyperstimulated follicles—ironically, the whole premise of in vitro fertilization. When one of those follicles burst, it caused the artery in my ovary to bleed into my abdominal cavity. Which explains why nearly thirty percent of the blood in my body was gathered there. Had they not been able to give the blood back to me, to redisperse it into my veins, I would have gone into shock.

You and Mom looked ashen. You didn't leave the hospital until after 11:00 p.m., a sixteen-hour day. I came home the next morning blackened and bruised, grateful to be all right but distraught over what had happened, this unexpected event that could derail everything hopeful we had worked toward since your diagnosis. I didn't believe the doctor when he told me I still might be able to have the embryo transfer that Sunday. It seemed impossible that my body could sustain a pregnancy after all this trauma. "Let's just see, let's be hopeful," he said.

Frozen Peas

I HAD EXPLICIT INSTRUCTIONS WHEN I LEFT THE
hospital to put frozen peas on my crotch. "Do it as often as you
can stand it," one of the nurses told me. "You want to bring the
swelling down."

You got two bags of Bird's Eye peas, and for the next two and a half
days I had a freeze-a-thon on our black leather couch. I looked like
something otherworldly, with a coconut for a groin. I was so engorged
and sore that I couldn't sit in a straight-back chair. Everything
throbbed, right down to my toes.

Those first twenty-four hours were critical, since we had to
return to the IVF clinic the next morning. As long as the bleeding had
stopped and the swelling had gone down, the doctor would allow me
to have the embryo transfer. With all that we'd been through—your
drama and mine—the least I could do was suffer frostbite.

I prayed, with one bag of Bird's Eye peas, and then, when it
turned warm and mushy, I sat with the second bag, fresh from the
freezer, crinkled and firm. Over and over I said my mantra of wellness
and conception.

"Use the Krazy Glue method," I demanded of the doctor right
before the embryo transfer. He gave a half-laugh with a closed smile.

Four embryos were of high enough quality to implant. Still swollen, bruised, and scared, I asked, "How about putting in five embryos?" No, it wasn't safe, the doctor told me.

Bless the Food Network

WE WAITED FOURTEEN DAYS TO LEARN WHETHER or not we were pregnant.

You went to work. Between the hormones I'd pumped into my body over the past few months and the laparoscopy, I was exhausted. I don't think I worked at all those two weeks; such was the ebb and flow of the freelance world. The first week after the transfer I still couldn't sit in a hard chair or hold a pitcher of water. The swelling was nearly gone, but my pelvis remained blackened like a Cajun fish.

I lay on the couch and watched the Food Network for hours: Ina Garten, Emeril Lagasse, Bobby Flay, Mario Batali. The chefs fed my spirits with saffron and chocolate, penne and sausage. It was easy to picture myself in the confident worlds of their kitchens, where only fragrance, color, and a panoply of tastes prevailed. They took away my inner fears like trusted friends, bathing me in sustenance.

Finally, November 16, 2000, the day when we would learn our pregnancy results, came. Not wanting to be jostled on the subway, I took a taxi to your office, where we called the clinic. Regardless of the news, we wanted to be together. I remember the way you closed your office door, and then came to take my hand. "Are you ready?" you asked. I was. And so were you.

You put the phone on speaker so that after a brief yet interminable hold, we heard a joyful "Congratulations" from the nurse. "We're so happy for you." I might have tackled her had she told us in person.

Instead, we gripped each other in a long, supportive embrace. You wore khaki pants and a sports coat, your back turned to a cityscape of tall buildings and yellow taxis racing across midtown Manhattan. I was crying and so were you. The softest tears of relief. I didn't want this miracle moment to end. At last we had reason to believe again that happiness could come our way. That night we settled on a boy's name. We stretched out on our bed and imagined. If the baby was a girl? You didn't like my suggestions. One by one you said, "Nah. Nope. No. Definitely not. Maybe. Hmm." We had a good laugh. Then I conceded, "Okay, I'll buy a baby naming book tomorrow."

Unfamiliar Territory

GOOD THINGS HAPPEN IN CLUSTERS. Bad things do, too. It's inexplicable to me why this is so, but everything in my experience upholds this truth. My pregnancy was carving a sunnier path.

First, I was offered a six-month assignment in the research department at *Working Woman*, my first on-deck job at a magazine. I had been dabbling in freelance writing and wanted to do more. My job was to cull facts for a special annual issue called "The Top 500 Women-Owned Businesses." I enjoyed the simple routine of calling the businesses, researching executive salaries, doing the occasional interview, and then plugging all that information into a ready-made template. My co-worker, Lia, and I shared a tiny office and ate potato chips every day at lunch. This was the magazine's flagship issue, one that branded them, and it felt good to be part of this large effort.

I didn't want more responsibility in my professional life; I just wanted to quietly do a job and collect a paycheck. Although I was wholly content to be a fact-checker, somewhere along the way, without any real effort on my part, I landed a writing assignment for the issue, a spread about women billionaires. It happened with so little fanfare that I couldn't help but think my world was being reordered. *It would be years after you died before I realized that I had a defining hand in creating such opportunities, that for my own survival, I put myself in new situations to tip the scales in my favor. Show up, participate, grab at life as though it's your last day.*

You were also feeling optimistic about your new job as a vice president at Businessweek.com. McGraw-Hill had recruited you after the demise of Pathfinder, and because you, too, felt deflated by its failure and the fact that many of your colleagues had moved on, you embraced the change. Different brand, similar digital landscape. Your energy was high. I noticed the way you buttoned your dress shirts faster each morning, with nimble fingers. And how your feet seemed to glide into your loafers and give a little pop when they touched the wood floor. You put your tie on with one fluid movement, kissed the tender, center spot on my forehead the way I loved, and went to work, confidently riding the subway.

People still stopped to stare at the back of your head. The baseball cap hid all but the lowest part of your skull, the part with a thick, carved line like a miniature trench, and an oval patch of skin taken from the inside of your leg to seal the original incision from your surgery. The two skins were different shades. Your looks would always scream "cancer patient" since your hair would never grow back to cover the scars and you weren't about to wear a toupee, or a wig, or have an implant. When Rogaine failed to work, we let things be. The stares continued—at the office, when we walked the city streets, went out to dinner, were anywhere in public—and while we couldn't change the way others saw you, I noticed a shift in the way you viewed the outside world. You gripped my arm and focused on the path ahead. No, you weren't as detached as you once were, not nearly as disconnected from people who made you feel an altered man. "How are you?" you'd ask with sincerity. Now there was a certain acceptance in your manner born from inside of you, from a place of hope and possibility after the tempest of three years ago.

The sweetest news came to us five weeks after learning we were pregnant. "I see two heartbeats," the doctor said. "You're having twins." You looked at me with such love and bliss in your eyes. Carrying twins felt like we'd been given a winning lottery ticket, this time on the right side, the upside, of life.

Grasping for the Winning Ticket

YOU CAN'T HELP BUT JUMP INTO A PREGNANCY when you have in vitro fertilization. Nothing about the process is organic or gradual, so you might as well get a running start. From day one, I owned my pregnancy. I bought maternity clothes long before I had to and caressed my belly even when I felt nothing stirring. The world felt lovelier now that I was carrying life inside—the sky seemed to have turned a more vivid blue, the sidewalks appeared freshly gleaming, and the sweep of city buildings stretched out like an unending grid of dominoes. Food tasted better, and I ate plenty of it now that I was eating for three and wasn't the least bit nauseated.

Which is not to say that I was worry-free. As good as I felt, as hopeful as life now seemed, I was jolted by unexpected moments of terror, the viciousness of it shocking to me still. Starting with the subtlest twitch in my eyebrows, panic moved over me like a choke hold, until it eclipsed everything good in our lives. It rose from nowhere but frailty, hitting me worst in the nights, when I woke to my own alarm, thinking you were gone, dead. Some nights your cancer had returned to finish you off. Other nights you simply disappeared without warning. Sometimes I dreamt that I miscarried again, this time later in the pregnancy, when my trust in motherhood had become real. Still other nights I imagined that one twin robbed the other of life. Many nights it was my own mortality that startled me awake: I had recurring, sweat-filled thoughts that *I* had cancer, that *I* would die. And then there were random, nonsensical dreams of a high school acquaintance caught dismantling our bathroom, pulling the toilet from the wall in search of an antique vase (*which we never had*), and of our casually giving away the son we'd always wanted at a friend's wedding. The most bizarre dream involved Abraham Lincoln instructing me to jump off a watchtower hundreds of feet high in order to save the Jews. In the dream I woke up in the hospital badly bruised and with epithets carved into my body; you and Abe Lincoln stood over me, thanking me for a job well done.

At the root of all this pregnant anxiety was the distorted thought that somehow we weren't deserving. I fought hard against these feelings, talking them out with my mom, who painted her dreams and tried to make sense of mine. "You're afraid things will be taken from you," she'd say. "It's understandable. But remember, honey, you are in control of your thoughts and feelings."

I also went to see a favorite social worker from CancerCare who had helped me after your diagnosis. You're having post-traumatic stress, he said, nonchalantly, as if I ought to have expected it, which made me feel a little stupid. "It's normal and it's real." I remember the way he emphasized the word *real*, saying it slowly and drawing out the *l* so that it lingered on his tongue and in the air around us. Having a legitimate diagnosis allowed me to box my fears into a more confined space in my brain, so that they weren't so sprawling and scattershot. "Your confidence will return, kiddo," he told me. The prescription? A simple mantra I could use as often as needed: *Body calm. Body quiet. Body open.*

Days were better. I said the mantra often, first thing when I opened my eyes each morning and from my tiny perch at *Working Woman* magazine. I managed to get through the hours this way, even if some days the words were like vapor. Each time this happened, the muscles of my heart tightened, bringing a fresh wave of anxiety. So I started all over again, like a student who is desperately trying to learn the English language. I needed that winning ticket.

Throughout my pregnancy, my fears grew as large as my belly, bigger even than the two lives swimming inside.

Quiet Reverence

EVERYTHING ABOUT MY PREGNANCY FELT NEW. Spring was here and with it a gentle hum from the neighbors taking time to greet one another on the tree-lined street beneath our windows. Our love, too, felt deeper and sturdier, the embattled ship finally moored. The gift of life, *this* is what we were feeling.

When I wasn't working, I busied myself looking at baby furniture. We'd need two cribs, but I wanted a single dresser for now. Neither of us felt compelled to know the twins' genders; as long as everything continued to go well, we wanted to be surprised, this in itself a turn in our thinking to allow for the unknown. I splashed shades of green on their bedroom wall: celadon, bright apple, and yellow-green.

We splurged on a mini-vacation to Little Dix Bay. The idea of going somewhere new appealed to us.

Remember how you loved the ocean? The way you used to sit and watch the boats at the Southport Harbor, near your parents' condominium in Connecticut? With your Olympics baseball cap slung backwards over your head, you sat in silence on the weathered bench or on a patch of grass staring at the blue-black waves that rippled beneath the white and wood hulls. The peace of it filled you.

This is my enduring memory of our time in Little Dix Bay: the contentment on your face, the ease of your body sitting in the low beach chair, your legs loose and golden as the water splashed over your calves. You wore sunglasses a shade darker than the teal water, and on your iPod you listened to Springsteen's "Born to Run" with quiet reverence.

As you looked out toward nowhere in particular, I remember standing beside you, my belly hard under my red and white polka-dotted maternity suit. The top of the bathing suit flapped softly in the breeze. I wore a large straw hat and had had my toenails painted red. I was heavier than I'd ever been in my life, close to 180 pounds of baby, arm, and tush fat. But I was happy; the weight anchored me. And in that moment it anchored you, too, because my shadow covered you like a long wrap. Watching you in your state of oceanic bliss warmed me so much that I reached for your shoulder to lower myself onto the sand beside your chair. The sand was soft and creamy like wheat flour. I grabbed your hand and held it against my cheek, always our way of saying, "I love you." Had you left it there longer I could have slept on that husband hand of yours.

They Were Only Sand Sharks

THAT MORNING AT BREAKFAST YOU'D COMPLAINED
of a headache over your right eye. You were quiet as you ate your
pancakes. "Have some more coffee," I said. "The caffeine should help."

It was our last day of vacation, and like all the days before
we spent it on the beach. We found two lounge chairs beneath an
umbrella and plunked our towels and books and music beside us.
You dozed while I read.

An hour passed before the wind roused you and you opened
your eyes and yawned. Is there anything more relaxing than
sleeping on a beach? I looked lazily at the comfortable smile on
your face. "Love you," I said.

"I love you, too, babe."

"Sharks," someone yelled. "Sharks."

You popped up to join the gathering crowd in the water. I stayed
behind, but then you motioned me to come. "They're only sand sharks,"
you said. "Cool," yelled eager beachgoers as the three-foot sharks
dodged them. I stood on the sand, ready to bolt if necessary.

Why was no one moving from the water? I couldn't understand
it. Sharks are sharks.

You wanted me to go into the water with you later. "It's our last day," you pleaded. The water was warm, the sands sharks gone, and dozens of people swam amid bobbing waves. "Come on, I'll protect you." You held out your golden arms, and in spite of my fear I walked toward you. Don't be a ridiculous chicken, I told myself. I left marks on your skin, but I let you hold me close to shore.

Just Like Any Mother

IN APRIL IN MANHATTAN, LIFE BLOOMS. I felt healthily pregnant and treated myself often to walks in Riverside Park. As much as I walked this route—north to Grant's Tomb on West 122nd Street and then back again—I never tired of feeling the same cobbled stones under my feet or counting the sparse trees lining the road. Seven. Eight. Nine. Sometimes I could see a barge crossing the Hudson River. Other days, I simply concentrated on the buildings to the east of Riverside Drive, those with the gentle arches that had once accommodated horse-drawn carriages. The horses had been gone for decades, but it felt magical to me that the architecture remained. Looking at block after block of these buildings gave me a sense of permanence, and history.

My favorite pregnant-lady spot was the tot lot on 104th Street, not quite two blocks from our apartment. I couldn't help but smile each time I walked by and saw children playing on the climbing bars. On clear afternoons, when the sun warmed my shoulders, I sat with a book on the chipped green bench, casually watching young mothers or nannies make sand pies with their children in the sandbox. I watched toddlers take wobbly steps as their mothers followed close behind. "Just like drunken sailors," as my grandmother might have said.

I sat with my stomach bulging over my thighs, occasionally patting my mound of babies while making small talk. "Where do you live?"

"How old is your little boy?" "She's just adorable."

All these niceties rooted me to motherhood. Soon, at the end of July, I would belong to this world. I pictured myself pushing the twins in a pretty blue carriage around the tot lot. They would sleep while I told them what was happening in the playground. That so-and-so had thrown sand, that so-and-so hung upside down for four seconds, that so-and-so made it down the slide but fell at the bottom, not realizing she had to use her legs to prop herself upright. I imagined strangers in the park stopping to admire the babies, commenting, "Oh, how sweet, twins." They'd ask me how old the twins were and how we were managing the sleepless nights. "Well, good luck to you," they'd say with kind smiles as they stepped away from the carriage. In all these dream moments, I was a calm mother, a present mother, a woman who wanted to fuss over her children the way any other mother might do.

I Was Planning Ahead

MY ASSIGNMENT AT *WORKING WOMAN* MAGAZINE ended mid-April, ideal timing for me to tackle a few home projects before the twins' arrival. Each day I made lists about what to purge in my paper-filled office: old files, those darn Post-it notes, loose pages from three-ring binders. I felt a visceral need to do away with the haphazard clutter before the babies came. I'd start here, eventually getting to the closets and kitchen. Maybe I'd even clean the freezer, a job I hated but for some reason you noticed. "Look at this freezer," you would say as you dug beneath last night's chicken looking for the chocolate ice cream. I vowed to turn our home into a vessel of order, the secret, I figured, to a calm mind.

This calm, it worked in short intervals—nothing more, nothing sustained.

The problem was not the apartment. In spite of my concentrated efforts, I could not trust the order. Which was unfortunate, since harmony was the very thing I wanted. Nights were hardest, my dreams still vivid and surreal, always involving danger. When I woke, it was the same: I looked for you. Were you still breathing? Were you healthy? Would your cancer return? I remember bargaining with God, suggesting that if the cancer *had* to come back, it could wait until the twins were fully grown.

I would never have revealed these fears to you, since speaking them aloud might have given them life. Yes, any expression of doubt could have shifted our delicate reality; as long as I battled the demons on the inside, they had less chance of escaping into the open, less chance of becoming real.

Imagine this false superstition I felt. As if I could actually ward off evil. As if I could cause you to get sick through the spoken word, and then strike a deal to prolong your life.

There was more to it than my own morbid premonitions. God forbid I give you reason to doubt again when you were feeling so positive. You had no trace of cancer beyond your baldness, scarring, and unsteady gait. And for as long as we'd been married, eight years already, you'd dreamt of fatherhood. You couldn't wait to tenderly hold your children against your chest. You felt them before they were even born. This is the very image that germinated for you, the only future you saw.

I was also focused on the future, although mine looked different than yours. My future had been broken, the seams not glued together well. I had no idea how to resume life as usual, pretending as if nothing had happened.

But everything was good now.

You went to work and I stayed at home, making our space ready for the twins.

Slowly, the apartment was being purged and reordered as I'd hoped. Each time I opened the refrigerator to find the ketchup and mustard side by side, or saw your dress shirts sorted by color, or laid another unread magazine onto the neat stack beside our bed, I fought the sure feeling of dread—of a vague but foreboding loss. I felt it everywhere.

You Went for an MRI

BECAUSE YOUR MRIS HAD BEEN CLEAN FOR A year and a half, and you were otherwise healthy and feeling strong, you now went for brain scans every six months. Time off for good health. This MRI was just routine. "It's going to be fine," you reassured me the night before. You kissed my forehead four times—one for me, one for you, one for each twin. "Be positive. I feel great, honey."

And you were. Great. You were a man in your mid-thirties trying to move forward after a horrible scare. "Hopefully just one blip over the course of your life," Uncle Harvey said.

That night I planned your funeral in my dreams.

Thirty Weeks

I WOKE UP ON MAY 19 TO HEAVY SPOTTING. I was only thirty weeks pregnant. "Let's take a look at you," my ob-gyn said. He'd been at the hospital since the middle of the night and would wait for us to arrive. We found a taxi, nervous but confident that the bleeding was caused by pressure on my cervix. My doctor had warned us about this common possibility with twins. You held my hand the entire cab ride.

"Do you think I'll still be able to make my baby shower?" I asked the doctor when he examined me. Friends were hosting it that afternoon. We'd called it off on the way to the hospital but could easily reverse the decision. The team checked the babies' hearts, measured my cervix, saw that my pulse and blood pressure were fine, and observed two active babies on a sonogram. Two hours later, when they felt confident that all was well, my doctor said, "Yes, you can go to your shower. There's nothing to warrant keeping you on bed rest."

It meant a lot to me that my college friends Ellen and Nancy were throwing a baby shower. They'd been there for me, for us, before your diagnosis and for everything that followed—your surgery, treatments, and road to recovery. You delivered me to Ellen's apartment, chatting with our friends before heading out with the husbands for a beer.

I was bloated and uncomfortable, anxious about spotting again but trying hard to be present at my own party. My friends were reassuring, hovering around me with food and water. I would be among the first mothers in the group, and the first to have twins. Everyone had questions; everyone was excited. "No, we still don't know the genders. We're going to wait, we've got two months yet," I teased. We sat in a circle in the living room and talked about our mates, our jobs, our days, but I couldn't quite relax.

Five minutes after I returned home, the gush of water came so urgently, so unexpectedly that I hardly knew what had happened. I screamed for you to come. "Quick," I said. I was standing near our bed. You rushed toward me, eyeing my wet pants and the fresh water stain on the oatmeal Berber rug, a look of pure shock across your face. "Do you think it's pee?" I asked.

Neither of us knew what to say. What did we know? We hadn't even started Lamaze class yet. I reached for the phone to dial our doctor.

He called back less than three minutes later. "What's going on?" he asked. I heard the worry in his voice. We had to get to New York–Presbyterian, the same hospital we'd visited that morning, right away.

"Kiddo," he said, less than an hour later, "your water broke. You're having these babies today."

Can't This Wait?

"GIVE ME THE DRUGS!" I screamed early that evening. "I want the epidural. I want the spinal. *Now!*" I was sweating like a woman possessed, my labor pains like jagged glass against my abdomen. I lay naked on the white bed except for the thin paisley hospital robe draped loosely around me. My rants went on for what felt like hours since I was slow to dilate, even after the Pitocin.

You tried to calm me. But it hurt too much to be touched. You stood by the bed for much of the evening because you wanted to be right there to hold me if I needed you. My writhing didn't scare you; you knew the pain would pass. You were excited about the birth.

A parade of nurses and technicians moved in and out of the linoleum room we'd been assigned, and at some point, a doctor in hospital scrubs came and pulled up a chair. He was one of the neonatologists. He had a stern face and a clipboard that he kept referring to while speaking to us.

It's nearly impossible to process substantive conversation in a state of distress, but this automaton doctor seemed intent on making me do so. You, too, although for some reason he kept looking at me. He was there, he told us, to share statistics about babies born prematurely. He might as well have faded into the cream walls behind him while rattling off survival rates: how babies born before thirty-two weeks of gestation who weigh less than three and a half pounds...

He'd lost me right there.

"Can't this wait?" I pleaded. It was necessary, he said, to talk—something about hospital policy. How dare he talk to me about survival? How dare he stress me more? How unfair, to be in labor while having to think about underdeveloped lungs and apnea and ventilators, to have to talk about infections and long-term disabilities like mental retardation, cerebral palsy, vision and hearing problems. It was too much.

I could have punched him.

You didn't say anything. You were equally unnerved.

The Best of Both

THERE WAS ONE UNEXPECTEDLY GOOD THING about my delivery: it was vaginal, far more rare with multiple births, and healthier for the babies' lungs.

"It's a girl," our doctor said, proudly holding her up for you and me to see. He'd known this beforehand, of course, yet respected our wish to keep the genders a secret. Everyone took such care not to tell us the sexes that the whole thing seems odd to me now (does it really matter?). I have a vague memory of the doctor putting our daughter against my chest, though not for more than a few seconds, since she was quickly whisked away to be examined.

The image of you looking at our seconds-old daughter under the fluorescent lights is one that still lingers for me. You gazed at this tiny creature with such reverence, as though you couldn't believe you were witnessing this moment. You couldn't believe that she was here. You never said so, but part of me always felt you couldn't believe you were here to see it.

Six minutes passed, a length of time I wouldn't remember at all, before our son was born. He shot out of me so fast that the doctor nearly dropped him. "Whoa," the doctor said, falling back on his feet to properly support this squirming bundle of slippery flesh. We'd laugh about this incident each time we told the story of Casey's birth. How he couldn't wait to enter the world. He was the twin who burst my amniotic sac with his kicking and shimmying.

It was after 1:00 a.m. on May 20, 2001. A Sunday. You called both sets of parents from the waiting room to share the good news. They were in their beds, in Connecticut, waiting for the call.

You looked tired, yet proud.

We Named Her Rebecca

WE NAMED HER REBECCA GRACE. At two and a half pounds, she'd already won her first fight. She had worked so hard to free herself from the birth canal that she wound up with severe eggplant-colored bruises on the left side of her face, shoulders, arms, legs, neck, and back. Hours later, her left eye blackened and swelled. It was uncomfortable to see her this way—where was my downy newborn? But she was breathing, stable, otherwise unharmed. "It will be all right," the nurses assured us. "The bruises will fade."

I had never seen a baby this little (less than the weight of a roasting chicken). You thought she was the most beautiful creature you'd ever laid eyes on. "My girl," you said to her, over and over.

He Looked like Elvis

HE DID, LOOK A BIT LIKE ELVIS PRESLEY, WITH those long, dark sideburns. Where did they come from? I wondered. Casey was the bigger twin: he weighed three pounds, two ounces, a larger "roasting chicken" than his sister but still the weight of a chicken. He was blanketed in soft hair, like velvet fuzz, and his spine was long and slender. I had the feeling that he would be tall.

We'd been forewarned that boys are less mature than girls at any gestational age, so it wasn't a surprise that Casey had difficulty breathing on his own. Right away he was fitted with oxygenated nasal prongs to boost his airflow. The prongs helped, but he needed more assistance. We weren't there to witness him grunting, a sign of respiratory distress, but that is what the nurses told us he began to do. He was placed on a ventilator with a tube the width of macaroni down his nose that pumped air through his trachea and into his lungs. A full-size baby might have moved his body more, possibly dislodging the foreign object in his air path. But not our three-pound son. He seemed soothed by the ventilator's low-frequency, rhythmic hum.

The First Day

I HAVE LITTLE MEMORY OF MY OWN BODY HOURS after giving birth—surely exhausted, puffy, sore, dry-mouthed, and with swollen feet. I must have been full of adrenaline because my body was not my concern. I was a mother now, and I needed to know that my children were well. They'd been taken from me seconds after birth, removed from the delivery room to the twenty-four-hour care of the neonatal unit. It was disturbing, like a dislocation, to have my just-born babies, children who grew inside of me for thirty weeks, who my own body had fed and sustained, suddenly be carried away by strangers, nurses wearing yellow gowns and plastic shower caps, while I lay sweating on a stretcher.

Sometime before the sun rose (I vaguely remember it being 4:00 a.m.) you pushed me in a wheelchair from the recovery room to see the twins. They'd been taken to room nine, one of four rooms in the neonatal unit, which they shared with eight other newborns. I sat with heavy legs, a thin film of sweat covering my skin, my face pale, looking with a mixture of terror and wonder through the prisms of the incubators at the tiny lives I'd just created. You'd already staked out the territory, visiting the twins when I was in the recovery room, and you were eager to show them off to me. We sat watching one twin, and then the other, for many minutes. Everything was still hazy for me, but it was miraculous to see them alive. It sounds foolish to say, but I remember thinking, *Yes, they are real.*

The morning passed uneventfully enough. Our parents drove in together from Connecticut, ecstatic first-time grandparents. We'd prepared them for the facts that the twins didn't look like full-term babies and that they were in incubators. "You can't hold them," we said. Whatever fears our parents had, they kept to themselves. They stared and stared at their newborn grandchildren, amazed that after so much struggle the twins were finally here, the perfect combination of one boy and one girl. Each had ten fingers and ten toes; all would be well.

We shared a deli lunch. I was hungry, ravenous actually, after the night's labor, and the food was a salve, as always, for my jittery nerves. My dad joked about my appetite, even though he loved to see me eat. "You take after me," he'd say, putting more sandwich in his mouth, too.

Our families left right after lunch, and you and I went back downstairs to check on the twins. This would be our role as new parents—the only real role we could play. One of the nurses kindly suggested that we get some rest; the twins, she said, were doing fine. We were exhausted, yes. "We'll come again later," we said. You placed your arm protectively around my lower back—I was unsteady on my feet—and we walked this way through the labyrinthine halls and up in the elevator to my room.

"Lie down with me," I said. So you did, both of us squished between the bed's raised rails. You wore your cotton, navy V-neck sweater, soft and familiar to my skin. I nuzzled against your neck, the way I did when I wanted to be close to you. *Your neck was smooth as linen; it was my favorite place on your body, the place where I smelled your goodness and love deeply.* We were so quiet together, in the first moment of stillness since the babies' birth. *We were parents. We were parents.*

At some point, we fell asleep, my head supported by your neck, your arms around me.

Collision

WE LAY TOGETHER IN A GROGGY STUPOR, SLEEPING but aware, too, of being in a hospital with its attendant sounds. I can't say for how long we rested. It was late afternoon, about 5:00 p.m., when your cell phone rang and you sprang up to remove it from the front pocket of your jeans. Your sweater was rumpled from sleep.

"Hi, Dr. Balmaceda," you said, looking at me as if you'd been struck by lightning.

Your heart, it must have coiled and stopped as you held the phone against your cheek.

You didn't rush to tell her about the twins' birth, as I might have done to divert the conversation. You were silent, listening. She had news.

Our cocoon of calm was broken.

In one heavy motion, you sat down on the bed, turning away from my hypervigilant ears, already on the highest alert.

"What is it?" I'm sure I yelled out to you.

Your MRI. The cancer was back.

No, this cannot be real.

I could tell that she was making arrangements for you to have more tests done. But when? *We just had two babies.*

You hung up the phone, your face frozen. With your head down, you told me that the scan showed a tumor in your brain and at least one in your spine.

Silence. Shock.

I was sitting up, my body electric on that coffin of a bed. You avoided my eyes. How could you face me, your wife who was still in the dawn of her motherhood?

"It's in your spine?" I questioned, not able or willing to believe what had just been said to me in the plainest of words.

More silence.

This was terrible, we both knew, that the cancer had grown into your spine. It could happen with medulloblastoma, your tumor, but why now? Why, after a full year of surgery, chemotherapy, and radiation (a lifetime dose at that), was disease spreading into your spine? Initially, you'd had one tumor, close to your brain stem. How was it possible that it had multiplied after all this treatment? *We made you cured, remember? You were supposed to be cured. Why else would we have had children?*

My mind shut down. I can't recall the immediate hysteria I must have felt, the betrayal, or the doubt that followed. Surely there was a mistake; the test should be redone. You were healthy, a father at last. Parenthood was our future—not cancer.

I do not remember the "we have bad news" phone calls to our families, or the way we must have held each other, with tears of disbelief running down our faces. I do not remember the way I might have clutched at you with my fists in tight, defiant balls, begging you to do something that you could not do: to take it back, to make your cancer disappear. *More like a child than the brave wife who would say, "Let go, Let go" seconds before you died.*

When I think back to this moment, when life collided with death, the abyss sucks me under. One moment we are on top of the mountain, having made the hard climb stronger and more whole. We stand appreciating the view until a vulture swoops down without warning and pushes us forward. We fall, and we keep falling.

It's only now, years later, that I feel your enormous bravery that day. It was your body, your life, your future dangling, yet when the twins were born, and in the weeks that followed, not even the threat of your own mortality punctured your will to embrace fatherhood. Fear dug your eyes deep into your skull, giving you a haunted look—but still you were concerned foremost about the children and me. "I'll do whatever I need to do to get better," you reassured me, over and over. You were sorry for everything.

It was all so haphazard, the ordering of our lives, the lack of divine direction, and our own human frailty. This is what unraveled us most. We felt that sense of vulnerability, of being disposable, impermanent, targeted.

Why, on a day of new life, were we staring into the rim of death? I didn't understand it then. I still don't.

PART TWO

The Other Side

Alone in an Empty House

MONDAY, MAY 21, 2001. This is the day I was discharged from the hospital, less than forty-eight hours after giving birth. Had I had a cesarean the doctors might have kept me longer, but since there were no complications after my vaginal delivery, off I went, a swollen, fraught mother bound for home without her newborn babies and without her husband. You couldn't bring me home from the hospital because Dr. Balmaceda had arranged for you to be at another hospital, New York–Presbyterian, for a spinal tap. Neither one of us thought to postpone the test; we simply followed the doctor's orders, your disease, once again, dictating our lives. The radiologist was slotting you in as an emergency case; it was critical to know whether individual cells had spread throughout your spine.

Ellen visited me that morning on her way to work. I have zero memory of this, but she tells me it's true, and that again and again, as if in a trance, I repeated the words "I don't believe this is happening. Why can't he bring me home?" I'm sure she felt as helpless as I did. What solace, after all, can a friend offer in such a situation? *It will be all right. Try not to worry.* Such genuine reassurances would have felt meaningless, insincere.

Two feelings remain sharp from that day: nausea and panic. Each feeling reinforced the other. The more anxious I was over your spinal tap, the more I wanted to retch. The more I wanted to vomit—to expunge all traces of illness from our history—the more panicked and desolate I felt. Adding to this drama were raging post-pregnancy hormones; my body steamed with sweat. I had started to pump breast milk, but the milk wasn't coming easily and my breasts were as painful as if a wood board was pressing down hard against my chest.

Sometime that morning I spoke to Julie, my college roommate from Colorado. We'd talked the previous day after the babies had been born but before your terrible news. Few times in my life have I cried as hard—like a cumulative wail of grief. The words—"The oncologist called; Brett's cancer is back"—were too much to tell, too much to hear. I have an exact image of the way my body convulsed on that solitary white bed, the way I was panting primal, harsh sounds that came from some unexposed cavity. The words and tears slurred together, unrecognizable even to me. It was the separation over the phone that allowed me to break apart the way I did. The phone felt safer, more distanced. No one, not even Julie, could see how such crude fear, shock, and anger had unhinged me. *Was I even human in such a moment?* Few times have I felt this fragile. *Not even at your funeral.*

I asked our neighbor and friend Marina to bring me home from the hospital. Our families were so fraught that it didn't occur to me to ask anything more of them. We were all strung out, hanging on by loose threads, trying to keep our sanity and optimism under such unthinkable circumstances. Marina says on the taxi ride home I obsessively fidgeted with the thin plastic tubes attached to the breast pump I was supposed to use. The nurses had instructed me on how to use the device—I'd tested it at the hospital—but now all maternal confidence vanished. *Whoosh.* Just like a brain seize when you cannot remember the very thing told to you seconds before. *How do I use this thing again?* Figuring out the breast pump was a worry but not The Worry, which was clear: your health.

Now what? I think, as Marina deposits me at home. She's concerned about me and heartsick about your news, but I promise her that I'll be okay. She lives only one floor below us with her husband and baby. I need her to leave even though part of me dreads being alone. What am I supposed to do, alone, in my apartment? I feel strangely dissociated from this space; its quiet emptiness rattles me. I have no idea when you'll return. Sometime this afternoon. But what if the spinal tap spells disaster and they decide to admit you at once? It could happen.

I'm still standing in the foyer when I see your breakfast dishes on the kitchen counter. As if in a trance, I walk toward them. You left a plate with muffin crumbs on it and a coffee mug with a layer of cold coffee. Life exists with this evidence, and it's enough to send me walking room to room. Slowly I pass our dining alcove and head toward the family room. There's the black couch and coffee table and armoire with doors open to the television set. Here are the two skinny area rugs in the hallway and the black-and-white photographs on the wall. My desk is the way I left it, with a heap of papers and files, Post-it notes and paper clips. I drop my hospital bag in our bedroom. The blue walls soothe my eyes. Our cherrywood bed is handsomely dressed in a plump down comforter, the same shade as the walls. I love this bedroom. But I don't want to rest now. I'm too agitated to lie down.

I push open the door to the twins' room, which is still unfinished, with splotches of paint on the white walls. I haven't decided on the color yet, but I'm leaning toward the bright apple green. There's no furniture in this room, not a dresser, couch, cribs, or bassinets. Just a large yellow stuffed duck with a pastel green bow around its neck that I received as a shower gift. The duck and a few items of clothing, also shower gifts still in boxes, are the only things I have for the babies. I have no laundry to wash for them.

How does one mother in an empty house with no babies or furniture or clothes? And where are you? I want to know. I'm growing impatient for no reason because I need you here with me right now.

It's time to pump milk. This, at least, serves some purpose. The only mothering I can do. I grab a glass of water and sit down heavily on the couch. I put my bare feet on the glass table for support. "You can do it," I tell myself, trying to connect the machine to the tubes to the suction cups to my two engorged, alien breasts.

A Strange Grace

THAT FIRST WEEK OF THE TWINS' LIFE WAS A strange grace period. A pause after the immediate crises of their premature birth and your recurrence. Your spinal tap was the only medical necessity that week; whatever other procedures and tests you needed would follow. The tap, it turned out, was negative, meaning the tumors were localized. Good news for now. You and I spent as much time as we could visiting our twins in the hospital, grasping at parenthood however we could.

There was much to learn about the neonatal unit: protocols about hand washing; the names of the nurses assigned to room nine; where to store my breast milk; and medical terms like *apnea, brady-cardia,* and *desaturation,* all of which are common (but still frightening) conditions related to a baby's respiratory pattern. I would startle each time one of the twins had an apneic episode, which meant that for a few seconds, maybe more, they stopped breathing. All these things that parents of full-term babies do not have to worry about for us became the language of parenthood.

Sometime that week, we received an unexpected gift of two teddy bears, one cotton candy pink and the other sky blue. An acquaintance who had delivered twin girls prematurely the year before had sent them. The bears were half the size of my hand, and it was our friend's suggestion that we place them inside the twins' incubators along with photos of the two of us. To symbolize family. We were learning; we would continue to learn.

When I think back to the early days of the twins' lives, I am struck by how you simply needed to be a father. You looked at those babies as if they held the secret to life. As though they were precious gemstones radiating healing energy—enough to sustain themselves, enough to cure you. It was both serene and painful to watch you watching them. The world slowed when you looked at them, so that everything became distilled. And in a way it was true; everything you needed at that moment was right there packed into thirty inches of incubator space. I remember thinking, *How does he do it?* Your calm was remarkable, and I envied it. I tried to share your stillness. I did. But I found it too hard to separate you as new father from you as dying husband—because in my mind, your cancer would certainly kill you. We just didn't know when.

Our babies were neither the smallest nor the largest in room nine. They weren't the sickest or the healthiest either. Both were born with blood infections, plus Rebecca suffered from a urinary tract infection from two different types of bacteria. I wasn't aware of it, but I must have had an infection in my own body that I passed along to them in utero, which explains why my water broke. A "spontaneous rupture of membranes," according to the neonatal report.

Every newborn there had a story. A baby boy steps from Rebecca's incubator born at twenty-four weeks needed heart surgery. And in the lobby I met a woman who had given birth to twin girls at twenty-seven weeks. One of the twins had a severe brain bleed and had nearly died.

This much I surmised: there was a universe of need in the neonatal unit, and for my own sanity, I had to detach from the daily, even hourly dramas around us. I forced myself not to peer at the other babies, wondering about the circumstances surrounding their births and if they would be all right. When two or more nurses hovered near a particular infant, I looked away. I focused on our own children, to parent and love them through the plastic domes of their incubators.

Do you remember how, with our index fingers, we learned to hold their feet? Sometimes, when they were positioned right, we even brushed those same fingers beneath their gossamer hands. Touch mattered, for them, and for us.

Breaking the News to Your Boss

YOU HAD TO TELL YOUR BOSS THAT YOUR CANCER was back. She was not the same boss you'd had when you were diagnosed because you had changed companies about the time we began trying to conceive. *Your longest period of wellness.* We had no idea how your boss or the management at McGraw-Hill would respond. It was a global company, and there were rules to follow. We hoped for compassion, as there'd been at Time. Did we rehearse a script you would use to frame the cancer in the most positive light? I can't recall. Later we would do this often.

You were nervous, queasy really, about telling the company, and though you didn't burden me with these fears, I intuited them. What if your boss insisted you take a medical leave? This would have shattered you emotionally, not to mention crippling us financially. What if she reduced your responsibilities? There were any number of unknown outcomes—starting with your life.

For now, McGraw-Hill was supportive. You promised to update them once you knew more about your treatment plan. You would keep your own schedule; no one would micromanage you. You were a vice president. You were always responsible.

The Palm of Your Hand

IT WAS HARD TO DESCRIBE JUST HOW TINY THE twins were compared to full-term babies. Together, they weighed less than the average newborn, less than the two-quart jug of syrup in our pantry. No one among our family, friends, or colleagues had ever had a preemie baby. Ours were the first, a shock to everyone's senses. Our friend Malaak told people that each twin was the size of her thumb. We laughed about this for many months. It was a ridiculous notion, of course, but if you looked at it through another lens, the foreignness of having children born so undersized and shriveled was real.

I wouldn't let anyone take pictures. It was too traumatic for me to see the babies this way, at "home" in heated incubators with tubes and bruises and cracked skin thin as glass. Some part of me was afraid that they might not survive. And photos... well, they had a permanency about them. You and my parents couldn't understand my hesitancy. "Someday you'll want to look back and remember just how far they've come," you collectively said. I relented only when we were finally able to hold them in our arms, day five for Rebecca, day seven for Casey.

When I look at those images today, they are like gold. We're seated in two adjacent chairs in room nine, each of us holding a baby dressed in a onesie and loosely swaddled in a white hospital blanket with teal and pink stripes. You hold Casey in the palm of your right hand. His whole body supported, right there in the curve of your palm. With your left hand you hold his head. I don't appear as confident holding Rebecca. I hold her with both arms in an awkward embrace.

The Dance of the Neonatal Unit

HOSPITALS ARE BREEDING GROUNDS FOR RISK, posing yet another worry about things beyond our control.

Every day at the neonatal unit produced a new routine of some sort, requiring us to learn the moves. Room nine, like all the rooms, bustled with commotion, with each baby on his or her own schedule, for feedings, blood work, tests, scans, procedures. The way the medical team managed it all was a feat of wizardry. I felt jittery being in this environment, my trust badly shaken, so that each time I walked past an incubator or oxygen tank, I worried I might fall against it and knock it to the floor, harming a baby in the process.

The twins—like the majority of the babies there—were on constant watch. Their heels and toes and fingers were pricked at least once daily, sometimes more, to check for infection, oxygenation, and blood gas levels. Those scars remain visible today as smatterings of white bubbles on their hands and feet. Before each change of shift, the attending nurse and doctor would assess the babies for septic shock, cardiac irregularities, the temperature and color of their skin, their bowel movements, the feel of their abdomens, their level of responsiveness and arousal, the color of their urine, the sound of their breath, and their overall degree of comfort or pain. All this took place several times a day and into the evenings, according to the reports. These tests were the ordinary checks and balances of the unit; anything "unusual," more common than not in an intensive care setting, required additional procedures and exams.

It's a wonder with such activity that the twins had time to nurse, something they couldn't do on their own since they wouldn't suck or swallow for weeks. Instead, they were fed through nasal gastric tubes that carried my breast milk and NeoSure, infant formula designed specifically for low-birth-weight babies. Exclusively breast feeding the twins was never an option.

We were all so busy dancing to whatever tune greeted us on a given day that I hardly found time to process the sadness I would come to feel about the twins' six-week stay in the neonatal unit. I worried about them, but the real mourning—that not even their births had come easily, and that they would live and you would eventually die—would come much later. Right now there was more breast milk to pump. And label with the twins' names and place in room nine's refrigerator. Double the pumping, double the milk, double the oddity of mothering in this fashion, on a shared refrigerator shelf with my twins encased in plastic bubbles.

I gravitated to one of Rebecca's nurses, a woman named Joyce with an incandescent smile. She took special interest in Rebecca, nicknaming her The Diva in response to her loud wails for attention. As frail as she appeared, my daughter had a piercing, shrill cry that we could recognize from across the room, where her twin brother lay in his own incubator, with his own nurses monitoring him.

Every time Rebecca cried, the nurses chimed in "Diva," smiling a little to themselves and one another at her feisty spirit.

"Don't you worry about her," Joyce would tell me in the volatile days to come, "she's going to be just fine." She gave me the same message on many days when she saw me crying. "He'll be all right. You'll see," she'd say, giving me a soft squeeze on the shoulder.

Six Weeks Passed

TIME SPENT IN HOSPITALS IS TIME STANDING still. One day bled into another, with weekends (for you), when you weren't working or at the oncologist's office, being the only clear delineation. There is something ironic about the way time passed so quickly because the moments within each day felt static. I never understood how it was that the days didn't end—sitting for hours in the neonatal unit exhausted me—but then suddenly over a month had passed and the twins were healthy and stable enough to leave. One day they had infections, one day their heart rates dropped, the next day, it seemed, we were preparing to welcome them home. By now, I no longer needed permission to pick them up. I was (mostly) comfortable holding them and, more important, nursing them from my breasts, which made me feel competent in my mothering for the first time since they'd been born.

Casey was discharged first, on June 27, 2001, the day after our eighth wedding anniversary. He was thirty-nine days old and weighed four pounds, seven ounces. When we finally left the hospital, you snapped his infant car seat into place, testing its sturdiness against the pull of the safety belt. "Ready, buddy?" you asked him, certain that he was secure. *What a fine father you would be.* You gave me a kiss before I climbed into the backseat next to Casey so that I could hold his head upright when the car moved, something I would do with both twins for months. You drove across town slowly and with such enormous pride that I half-thought you might announce to the cars around us, "Look at my son. I'm bringing him home today."

In spite of your cancer recurrence, and my fears about your survival, it was miraculous to have Casey home. I nursed him and you held him for what felt like hours on our green chair-and-a-half in the living room. The image lingers for me, because you would have held him against your chest for eternity if possible. You really loved to sink into that velvety chair.

We brought Rebecca home two days later. Smaller than her twin brother (more breakable in my mind), she weighed less than four pounds, just like a porcelain doll. I nearly dropped her when she threw up the next day—a terrifying moment that made me question my ability to care for these fragile infants. We had a baby nurse with us, and without even thinking about how to respond, I thrust Rebecca's writhing body into her sturdy arms. "Here, take her," I said, not even using the word *please*. I couldn't move my feet. *Paralyzed on the kitchen floor.* The whole episode was a matter of seconds, but to me, it felt like minutes without breathing. I watched the nurse calm my daughter against her chest, remove her soiled onesie, and then wash her in the kitchen sink, holding the baby's neck upright and cooing to her that everything was all right now. "She's just fine," the nurse assured me, looking over her shoulder to see if *I* was in fact all right. "Babies throw up, that's all."

It would take time to trust my instincts as a mother. To know what to do when the twins spit up, when and how much to feed them, how to bathe them, how to cut their nails, how to position them upright enough to quiet their reflux while supporting their necks, how to treat their diaper rash, how to start them on a sleep schedule, how not to panic when something seemed out of the ordinary, because babies, I would learn, are human beings who catch colds, run fevers, throw up, and cry for long stretches without provocation or reason. All "normal" aspects of babyhood. All "normal" things for a new parent to learn. They do not die from such things—something a parent whose life had not been jolted by cancer, whose husband was not dying in her mind, would never even imagine. The way I did.

What was not "normal" or expected was how all the physical labor—the bathing, middle-of-the-night feeds, laundry, rolling on the carpet, and later, chasing the twins at the playground in the park—would be done by me. You were being prepped for more chemotherapy, so right off the bat you couldn't diaper them, the risk of infection being too high (one of your few lucky breaks, we decided). You needed your rest in a different way than I did, especially since you went to work each day. It was just understood that you would sleep at night and I would feed the twins. While you were otherwise asymptomatic, your balance was still a problem, which made physical activities like kneeling to bathe the children an impossibility. These were real limitations that we would learn to work around.

Nothing would be the way we thought it would be. Not even the niceties we expected from others. Do you remember how bothered you were that none of our friends told us the twins were cute or beautiful or handsome the way people are supposed to do when you first have children? "We always told them *their* kid was cute," you said, half in jest, one Sunday on our black couch, when the babies were four months old. The compliments wouldn't come until the twins were nearly seven months, when their preemie skin had loosened and their bodies grown plump.

It feels wrong to say—certainly it doesn't reflect lack of love—but the twins really weren't adorable in those early months. It would take time for them to become supple with life, and for me to come into motherhood. There was so much to accept at once, caring for preemie twins fused with your new cancer regimen: the stem cell transplant, chemotherapy, surgery, and ultimately, when the twins were two and a half years old, and nothing else could be done for you, when you were suffering from seizures and delirium, *your merciful death*. No, I would not come into motherhood—in the sense that I felt real joy in being the anchor of my children's world—until the twins were five, long after they were babies and toddlers, long after you died.

Five Percent

UNCLE HARVEY HAD BEEN TALKING TO A COLLEAGUE of his at New York University, Dr. Jonathan Finlay, an expert in brain tumors who had done important work on medulloblastomas in children. You'd seen Dr. Finlay over a year ago, in the summer of 2000, for a consult after an indistinguishable blob appeared on your scan that he determined was probable scar tissue from your radiation (you'd had radiosurgery anyway so that they could zap it completely). But now, your cancer would require a more specialized, creative approach—"the cookbook method," Dr. Finlay would say, alluding to the way he would treat you with the maximum dose of one drug, a potent form of another, with still another active agent fed directly into your brain through a port called an Ommaya reservoir, beating, folding, simmering these concoctions until your body might rise up like the perfect soufflé. As loyal as we felt to Dr. Balmaceda, there was no doubt in our minds we'd go where Harvey felt you would receive the most aggressive care.

In many ways, Harvey was our voice. What did we know about any of this? As an oncologist, he questioned, weighed, consulted. As our uncle, he explained and comforted. He was the first person we called after your diagnosis (before our own parents), and he would be there, alongside us, until the end of your life. Whatever news we would receive from this point on—from bad to okay to worse to okay again to terrible—he softened, not by what he said (he would never distort the truth) but by his capacity for listening and understanding that seemed to transcend our pain, our fears.

Harvey flew in for that first meeting with Dr. Finlay. According to the notes, the day was August 20, when the babies were three months old. I had thought the visit took place when the twins were still in the neonatal unit. It surprised me to learn otherwise, although I understand it now, the way time collapsed.

Dr. Finlay was a pediatric oncologist, meaning that everything in his office from the kitty cat posters on the walls to the happy-feet carpet, bright green with a smattering of blue, yellow, and red shoes, had a childlike feel. This was strange for us, to move from the serious adult world of oncology to the pediatric ward, which was just as serious but for the playthings and children who laughed in spite of their cancer. Since your tumor primarily affected children ages five and under, you had to be treated where the expertise lay.

I remember the three of us—Uncle Harvey, you, me—sitting on the dark couch in Dr. Finlay's tenth-floor office. Dr. Finlay sat across from us, in an armchair in front of the large mahogany desk neatly stacked with folders of his patients. He had a mop of curly gray hair, a lilting British accent, genial and warm. He and Harvey were friends, peers, so in the beginning, the conversation was light. But very quickly, it was time to attend to business—the business of your life—and the tone changed. I remember the way Dr. Finlay moved in his seat, crossing his hands over your file, the one transferred from Dr. Balmaceda. He wanted you to know that he had a plan. "Listen carefully," he said, emphatically rattling off names of potential drugs, new drugs, with an urgency that bordered on excitement.

He spoke to you, to us, but only Harvey followed the discourse, the debates about one drug versus another and clinical trials. I took notes with no real concept of what I was writing. At one point I reached for your hand, longing for your touch in the midst of you being dissected like a specimen.

When it was all decided—your treatment plan set—you wanted

to know one thing: your odds of beating the cancer. "Five percent," said Dr. Finlay, his eyes holding yours in a level gaze. *Silence.* "But you, Brett," he said in the kindest tone, "you are not a statistic." *Pause.* "There is either all of you, or there is none of you."

The power of his words shot through me so that suddenly my body was pitched forward and erect. You didn't say a word. The air seemed to pulsate. No one had ever talked "statistics" before. I remember trying to digest the words. *Five percent.* Had I heard him correctly? Yes, that was clear by the way he was looking at you, trying to gauge your reaction. It was too late now to reframe the discussion, the words "five percent" filling the room with a power all their own.

In an instant, right there beside me on the couch, you went from being fully alive to near dead.

In the most physical sense, Dr. Finlay was correct: you couldn't half-exist. But those words, "five percent," I couldn't escape them. "Five percent" chance is what I told my parents and brother and close friends later that night. *Preparing for widowhood.*

Not you. You never mentioned the words "five percent" to anyone. You told your parents only that Dr. Finlay had a plan. That it would be a rough year, but you were up to it, and that we all hoped the combination of new drugs would work. It was stunning to me at the time—almost as shocking as hearing the words "five percent"—the way you avoided the bleak reality. "Were we not at the same meeting?" I asked. "Why aren't you telling them the truth?" *My* truth. Not your version, which left no room for "five percent." As though Dr. Finlay had never said the words. As though I had made the whole thing up. As though we spoke two languages: resolute patient with the Sisyphean task of beating the large odds of his disease, who for his own survival must deflect defeat of any sort, and broken caregiver, whose own plane of reality has been pierced, who cannot for her sanity, her own survival, trust in a positive outcome any longer. For what is the point? she asks.

I saw then—and I see now—that it was your right to want to live. No one could force you to accept a death sentence but you—and you were not about to desert your infant twins, who needed a father as desperately as you needed them.

We lived in these disparate realities until the last few months of your life, when the imminence of your death was inescapable to everyone.

A Hard Year

THAT WAS A TERRIBLE TIME, THE FIRST YEAR OF the twins' lives. We had beautiful, tender moments with them when we held them close and they slept in our arms, when they smiled, when they said their first words, Mama and Dada. Yet so much of that period was blighted by your illness. A full year of treatments and hospitalizations. And you going to work while trying to manage everything, keeping up a fighting front. And I fighting a different battle, the background static of your dim probability of survival.

Thanksgiving would have been a downer anyway, but as it happened, you were in the hospital with a blood infection and fever. I saw you earlier in the day and then traded places with your parents and sister, Marcy, who brought Thanksgiving dinner to you. So that I wouldn't be alone, my brother, Greg, came to the apartment, small turkey and stuffing in hand. The twins, meanwhile, feasted on rice cereal. I had always loved Thanksgiving until then.

You Bounced Back (Enough)

BEFORE WE KNEW IT, THE TWINS TURNED ONE. For the time being, your cancer was in remission, although neither one of us was foolhardy or naïve enough to think you cured, as we once had. You were in remission. And we could trust only the present. But since the present was calm, I, at least, felt freer to make plans.

First, we have a small family ceremony at our apartment to celebrate the twins' birthdays and give them Hebrew names. A two-for-one event. We give Rebecca the name Hadassah, or flowering tree, after Grandma Myrtie, who's there that day, as are Grandma Casey and your grandma Nettie. Casey is given the name Casrael, crown of God. A Rabbi friend we'd met during one of your hospital stays says a few prayers. It's generous of him and his wife to come since they lost their son to brain cancer the year prior. And Erik Kolbell coofficiates with wise words and a copy of the book *Oh, the Places You'll Go!* Everyone is buoyant as we pass the twins from arm to arm.

A few months later, we took the twins to Ocean City, New Jersey. You always welcomed the ocean, but the trip was my idea because I craved the semblance of a family vacation. *At least one.* The trip was poorly conceived. I underestimated the work involved traveling with babies. Little sleep. Little rest. No reclining in beach chairs tuned out to music or lost in a book. Crying babies who fussed in the sand but then tried to eat it anyway. I wanted the dream, not the reality.

One afternoon when the twins were supposed to be napping but wouldn't, we brought them to a nearby park, hoping the walk and fresh air would tire them. Another mother at the park admired them and without provocation told me that her daughter had been a twin. She pointed to her daughter, Mary, climbing up the jungle gym. I sensed something had happened, but I waited until you went for a soda and cookie across the street to ask her. "Joe died of a brain tumor two months ago," she said. "He was ten years old." I swallowed hard, frightened by what she'd revealed. And yet the calm on her face surprised me. I told her about your condition, each of us feeling compassion for the other. How was she managing? I asked. "He's with me all the time. It's like he's in another room."

I hoped that, when it was my time to mourn you, her bravery would rub off on me. She was the face of courage, this mother from Maryland, and I've never forgotten her words.

More and More

THE WORLD OF TERMINAL ILLNESS WAS NOT THE only world we inherited after the twins were born. Because they came so early, we also inherited the world of premature parenting. Neither appealed to us.

There was one advantage, however, and that was living in New York City, a place teeming with specialists—for cancer, low-birth-weight babies, and so much more. Before we even left the neonatal unit, we'd been advised that the twins would likely have "delays." How could I ever forget the miserable doctor who'd preached the gospel of preemie possibilities the night that they were born? He's the doctor whose tongue I wanted to slice off for the rant of terror he inflicted—potential surgeries, disabilities, learning issues. I remain bitter about this doctor over a decade after my children were born. It isn't his fault that he was simply doing his job, or that the twins were born at thirty weeks, or that your cancer returned. Still, I blame that man for casting a spell of uncertainty.

As it happens, the twins have had developmental delays. Nothing severe, thank goodness, a reality that I reminded myself of continuously on days when I wanted to whine and question "Why?" Why weren't they walking yet? Why were Rebecca's legs stiff? Why did Casey fixate on cars? And phones? Why was he restless in his own body?

From the beginning, I hated the labels. At eighteen months old, my fiery daughter was diagnosed with a mild case of cerebral palsy. The news shattered me—blow after blow. And yet, in the same way you weren't a statistic ("There is either all of you, or there is none of you," said Dr. Finlay), I try my hardest to be sure that Rebecca is not defined by a condition that renders her different. She has the determination of an Olympian, like her father. And we're lucky, yes, lucky, that her condition is mild enough for most people to ignore. Which is not to say that she doesn't have insecurities; she has plenty.

As for Casey, his delays have been subtler, less clear: sensory, occupational, visual motor, gross motor. It's no wonder he's suffered from anxiety—on top of having internalized his father's illness and death in real time. Those big shoulders of his trapped the little boy inside, so that at eight and nine he'd still want to cocoon himself in my womb, where he felt safe. He's a boy full of creativity and heart, the ultimate pacifist with the gift of empathy for the world.

Enough. We had a large circle of therapists who came to our apartment, people assigned and funded by the city of New York to help preemies reach their milestones. A real circus on some days. These devoted therapists worked with the twins from the time they were a year old until they turned five.

They were all wonderful, but I wouldn't have managed to hold it together without Jill Barbre, our social worker. I can still see her, sitting cross-legged on the kitchen floor in her dark corduroy overalls and bangle bracelets, waterproof markers and loose sheets of off-white paper spread before her. She had round cheeks, long hair the color of hay, and a voice that soothed like a feather brushing skin.

Jill spent hours of play therapy with the twins, drawing simple linear pictures in blue or black marker to illustrate what was happening. I held them on my lap while together we read: "Here is Daddy lying on a long, glass-covered bench that takes pictures of his brain. Here is Daddy receiving special medicine in his brain. Here are Mommy and Daddy talking to the doctor."

And later... "Here is Daddy dead."

Page by loose page, they clutched at the words and images with raw hunger, captivated to see the story of their lives read to them as a book. Even now, my heart clogs when I think about the terror they must have felt but could not speak. Rebecca's relentless clutching and whining. Casey walking on his toes, squirming, unable to be soothed. It all makes sense.

A Milestone

YOU WERE THERE TO SEE THE TWINS' FIRST
academic milestone: starting preschool. An important rite of passage
for parents in New York City. The angst of trying to place two children
at a reputable school, let alone the same school, was (and continues
to be) enough to drive many "normal" families beyond the outer
reaches of the city, to Westchester, New Jersey, or Connecticut. We
didn't have this option because you needed to be close to your doctors.
Jill Barbre had an indirect connection to Columbia Greenhouse
Nursery School, and after a lengthy application process—there and
elsewhere—the twins secured spots at this sweet, progressive school
that in your mind was "Ivy League" since it was essentially on the
Columbia University campus. Remember how proud you were telling
everyone that your twins were accepted into an Ivy League school?
It wasn't true, of course, but you, of all people, were entitled to gloat
with fatherly pride.

I felt very vulnerable the day the twins started school, September
11, 2003, exactly two years after the worst terrorist attack on U.S.
soil. No one living in New York City could help but feel the hurt on
a deeply personal level, but you were also in worsening shape. Your
MRIs were still clean, but you moved more slowly, spoke more slowly,
acted more slowly. All these signs I took as evidence that your disease
was back. I saw it in the pained look on your face when you tried to

sit in the twins' classroom during back to school night. The other parents moved aside to give you space, but it was nearly impossible for you to lower your body to the toddler-size chairs. And you had no energy to stand. I saw the strain, too, in the smudged shadows beneath your eyes. You looked like a man in agony.

So here we were, parents sending our children to school for the first time, side by side with other mothers and fathers who stressed over their children learning the alphabet or counting to one hundred. They talked about playdates, trips to the Children's Museum, and soccer in Riverside Park, and we stood by, rather helplessly, wanting to forge a place for our children among such normal company, trying to fit into these families' organized worlds, feeling more like pariahs than like friends. Cancer was not part of the preschool conversation, and the sight of you, I'm sure, was shocking to them since they were young and did not want to be reminded of their own mortality.

You might have gone back to the school once more, in the late fall for a parent-teacher conference, but mostly, you were absent from our children's new environment, either working a few hours or in treatment. Even when among the mothers at drop-off or pickup or somewhere in between on the walk to school, I felt an overwhelming sense of otherness. There was a lightness to these mothers that I wanted to absorb and emulate but couldn't. The wedge between us grew so wide that at times I felt clobbered by their unadorned joy and purpose. Eventually, I stopped trying to embody something I was not: a mother who never felt she had the time to linger and mingle and invest in building friendships or schedule parents' night out. Because I was not of them. And they were not of me.

Without my even knowing it, the year of preschool prepared me for the otherness I would feel as a young widowed mother.

It Didn't Make Sense

IN MY MIND MRIS WERE BLACK AND WHITE. Literally, black-gray meant normal and white (or shades of white) showed disease. It was November 2003, and in spite of your very obvious physical and mental decline, how you lost your balance and fell easily, how you were forgetting facts and people, how you kept thinking you were at the office when you were actually home, your brain scans revealed no evidence of disease. Nothing had shown up on the MRIs for months, not since your surgery at the beginning of the year. It didn't make sense, it didn't compute.

Which is how I came to see Dr. Stewart Fleishman, a psychiatrist who practiced hospice care and palliative medicine. I thought I was going crazy, watching you deteriorate before my eyes while the only concrete evidence we had—the MRIs—said otherwise. *This must be a chemotherapy reaction,* I thought. "He's fine, the MRIs say so," I'd tell myself with a stern shot in the arm as a rebuke for thinking the worst.

"Not true," said Dr. Fleishman. "You have to look at the whole picture, beyond the scans. You have to look at his functional abilities." He could see the way I was trying to bend the truth, the way I resisted hearing that you would eventually succumb to this disease. "Your husband will probably be on treatment for the rest of his life, which means that he will continue to show the cumulative effects of chemotherapy, the physical, emotional, and cognitive wear, even if his scans remain stable." Think of it this way, Dr. Fleishman told me, "the Brett you knew before cancer isn't coming back."

Was it wrong to admit that I wanted the old you back?

Paralysis Analysis

IN THE EARLY FALL I ATTENDED A SUNDAY SERVICE
with our friend Malaak, at Riverside Church. I'd come to Riverside
many times during off hours over the past few years to empty myself
under the arches that stretched toward the sky. Beyond the beauty of
the stained-glass windows, the splay of dark and light, and the neo-
Gothic architecture, it was the silence that spoke to me most. That I
could sit in such an enormous place—the tallest church in the United
States—and feel small and quiet within myself was transforming.
The minuteness of my presence allowed me to feel connected to the
sprawling space that surrounded me, and this, in turn, made me feel
part of the landscape, the city, the world.

We weren't affiliated with a synagogue at the time. You did not
believe in a God who would permit such a thing to happen to you—or
any person for that matter. You didn't tell me what to believe, what to
think; you kept to yourself. You were never religious, but your faith
was now in science, and you were still, at this point, hoping for a
medical miracle. I felt differently. While it upset me to see you reject
spiritual comfort, I was starved for contemplation, for the chance to
hear something that might lift me. Riverside was an interdenomina-
tional congregation with a broad social mission: I could take in what
resonated, letting more Christian notions wash over me.

I had no idea that the sermon would be called "Paralysis Analysis" on the day we attended services, or that the Reverend Dr. James Fitzgerald had prostate cancer that had metastasized to his bones. I had no prior knowledge that he would speak about living in the grip of cancer. "Human beings," he said, "are not hardwired to be paralyzed in this way and for such a long time." His words shot through me like an arrow. How was it that a man facing death could speak so philosophically, could rise above his pain? Paralysis was exactly the way I felt, and cancer or no cancer, it was no way to live. The reverend's message of self-empowerment was clear: we have the ability to redefine negative life events. Such a mission was beyond your will. But I could try—so that, for whatever time you had left, I would no longer be a prisoner of your illness. The service lifted me for days.

We Were Hanging On by a Thread

BY NOVEMBER, EVERYONE IN THE HOUSE — including you—was worn down, as though we were being suffocated. The twins were testing boundaries by climbing atop the kitchen counter, not listening, throwing things. Rebecca, who still banged her head on the floor when frustrated, ripped a favorite book, *When Sophie Gets Angry.* I don't recall the specific event that precipitated this destructive act, but it infuriated me (and also stopped me cold) that she would do this when the very point of the story was to show how Sophie learns to deal with her anger by climbing trees and looking out onto the world, thereby discovering the peace that comes from thinking more broadly about her problems. The twins loved when I read them the story—it calmed them—and now it lay in tatters on their bedroom rug. Casey, too, was wild, banging on his toy construction set, sticking his hands in his mouth, and running up and down the hallway with Cheerios-smattered hands to knock on our door, wanting you.

Parenting felt like a monumental effort. You were obviously still alive, still their father, even though you had no physical or mental energy to parent them. By now, it was almost impossible for you to stay on top of your job. You were still pushing yourself to dress and be at the office most days—*you so wanted to be a good husband and father*—but I saw the way you had declined cognitively and it terrified me. You needed help managing your workload and organizing your days. Looking back, I find it remarkable that you drove yourself the way you did and that McGraw-Hill allowed you to stay. They gave you plenty of space, but it was closing in around you now. Since your MRIs still read "normal," we did not yet inquire about long-term disability. But this would change soon, because in a matter of days, I had to write your performance review and help you recall very basic facts about what you did every day. "Your job is our job," I said in a rather soldierly way at first, a sick feeling in my stomach. The charade couldn't last. There was no way to disguise the fact that your brain had essentially gone out on you.

Another Thanksgiving passed. I yelled at the kids and found myself resenting the little things that you did not do. Like putting your socks in the hamper, or the dishes in the dishwasher, or making the bed. I focused on these things, these trifles, because doing so was easier than being swallowed whole by your cancer. I was drowning.

Finally We Had an Answer

IN DECEMBER YOU WERE SO WEAK THAT YOU staggered when you walked. I wouldn't remember the exact incident that led us to the hospital until I checked my journal and saw that you had taken a bad fall in our home. You fell and could not keep yourself upright again. It was as though you had forgotten how to walk.

I wouldn't even remember that you spent five days at the hospital, where a final MRI was done, revealing the worst possible news: your cancer had spread throughout your head in diffuse chunks of tumor. By then, Dr. Finlay had relocated to Los Angeles. I was with your parents when Dr. Sharon Gardner called. We had left you at the hospital moments before and were headed back to the apartment. Your dad was driving. Dr. Gardner had already consulted with Uncle Harvey, Dr. Finlay, and someone at Memorial Sloan-Kettering. All were in agreement that your options had run out. "There is nothing left that we can do but keep him comfortable," Dr. Gardner said.

At once your dad pulled over on a side street, and the three of us sat stunned and crying in the car. The news didn't surprise us—we knew you were dying before Dr. Gardner made it official—it was just that there was a finality to it, a sense of urgency, a dividing line we would be forced to accept.

I can't say for how long we remained in the car, or what words we said to comfort one another. But by the time we went home to face the twins, we had composed ourselves enough to be present for them. It was what they needed. It was what you would have wanted.

Hospice Came

DR. GARDNER MADE ARRANGEMENTS FOR HOME hospice care. You slept a good part of the day, sometimes until 2:00 p.m., but when you woke, you were often agitated about missing deadlines at work. On some level you knew that you had stopped working, and this knowledge must have shaken you deeply. You were obsessed with your PalmPilot and kept dotting at it with your finger. Many times you picked up your briefcase and said, "I'm going to work now." And then you would turn around and fall into the chair, thinking that you were at the office.

You also panicked about making the car payments and paying the other bills online; I tried to reassure you that you had already taken care of these things, that everything was done, but you wouldn't believe me. You were holding on tight to your last husbandly responsibilities.

Norma, our hospice aide, was built like a linebacker. She followed you around the apartment to catch you if you fell. You were wobblier than ever but refused to use the wheelchair or the walker hospice had provided. When you remembered to use your cane, you did, but mostly it seemed that you fought to claim whatever independence you could, even if it meant falling down.

"Stop treating me like an invalid," you lashed out one day.

Such clarity was rare. You'd been having mini-seizures that eroded the little cognition you had left. I never knew when they happened because they came unannounced, sometimes lasting only seconds. I could have been walking down the hall and missed one. Still, their cumulative effects were undeniable: your voice slurred and you were often disoriented. Sometimes you even hallucinated, imagining people in front of you who weren't there. In a way, these were moments of blessed anguish, because you were too sick to realize your own confusion.

Norma was an extra set of hands. When she wasn't trailing you, she loved to hoist the children in the air and swing them like sacks of rice. She played hide-and-seek and pretended to chase them, and they laughed and laughed. Music and life and death all at once.

At thirty-two months old, our twins were in constant motion, often running on opposite paths. They clamored for you. Casey, especially, loved nothing better than to climb all over you on the chair-and-a-half in our living room. He was the acrobat, and you were the good-natured (albeit pained) jungle gym. Usually I had to pry him away because your muscles were sore from atrophy and the play wore you out within seconds. It was both tender and sad to see the fierce, greedy love our son had for you. I remember the bad days, when he camped outside our bedroom door as you lay sleeping, this sensitive boy who would have given his soul for just one more day with his father.

The Bucket List

WE NEVER ACTUALLY CREATED A LIST OF LAST hurrahs. But our dear friends Nancy and Stuart wanted to get you one last cheesesteak before you died. You still had an appetite, probably from the steroids that you were taking to control the seizures. You had always loved cheesesteaks and for some reason were talking about them again. So one Saturday when Norma was off and my parents had the twins, Stuart and Nancy insisted on taking us to Philadelphia, home of the authentic cheesesteak. Stuart made a cassette with all your favorite music—Springsteen and Dave Matthews—to calm you on the rainy drive. Ever the New Yorkers, they researched the best venues and settled on two hot spots. We ate half a cheesesteak at one place, another half elsewhere.

Trekking a dying man two hours in a car to get a cheesesteak sandwich was both absurd and essential. We gave you a taste of life again. And you gave us a precious memory to hold.

You Collapsed over Vietnamese Food

EVER SINCE YOU WERE DIAGNOSED IN 1998, I HAD
wondered how you would spend your last moment alive. Would you
be conscious? Would you keel over in the living room of heart failure,
of all things, after years of toxic chemo treatments? Would you kiss
me good night and then die in your sleep, gray and motionless as
stone beneath the warmth of our pretty blue comforter?

As it happened, none of these predictions came true. Death, for
you, would be slow and unsteady, like your gait, except for the climactic
kicker, which hastened your demise one Thursday night in January
when the twins, mercifully, lay asleep in their apple-green room.

Norma had left for the day, so the house was ours again, an illusion
of family I clung to. The day had been uneventful for you—no
blinding headaches, no falls—so I invited our friends Sarah and
Wim over for Vietnamese food. Probably you said yes to please me,
since you knew that friends and family comforted me, their presence
a reminder of the circle of life surrounding us. You were very quiet
and, of course, confused, but on some level you registered that we
were still a couple and couples have dinner with friends. I remember
making a big deal about ordering from Saigon Grill, your favorite
take-out restaurant. We ordered all the dishes you loved: chicken
saté with peanut sauce, lemongrass pork chops, sticky rice, and some
sort of pineapple shrimp dish. I ordered before our friends arrived,

not knowing how long you would be able to stay awake. Often you fell asleep at the table, just dozed off.

You wore Levi's, a blue striped oxford shirt, and brown loafers, the ones faded around the toes from years of wear. You hadn't shaved in days, and circles the color of mud clouded your green eyes. Yet as you wobbled toward me in the foyer, I remember feeling a rush of love and awe. In spite of your clumsiness, the way you swiped the dining room column as you rounded the corner, I saw a certain grace in your determination, so that when you recovered your stance and smiled at me, my whole heart felt open. Your cancer fell away in that moment. Our friends had just arrived.

"I'm so happy to see you," I said, hugging Sarah while allowing myself to be held by her. Her cheeks, crisp from the cold, brought a heady whiff of fresh air and energy. You and Wim shook hands, and then Wim clapped you on the shoulder the way guys do when words fail.

We didn't linger long. The food had come moments before, so we made our way to the kitchen and helped ourselves to dinner right away. Sarah commented on how delicious everything looked. In better days, we'd have extended the evening, enjoying appetizers in the living room. We would have sat with our wine, perhaps a beer for you and Wim, facing each other on the black couch and armchair, relaxed and engaged in casual conversation about the Internet or the stock market or raising children or which Woody Allen film we liked best. But not tonight.

"Can I make you a plate, honey?" I asked, laying a steady hand over yours on the kitchen counter.

"No, I'll do it." You fixed your gaze on the food.

I struggled, allowing you your independence even as the social worker and hospice aides kept reminding me that dignity and self-preservation were vital. A terminal wish, to be able to dress and feed and go to the bathroom by yourself, as long as possible. So, in spite of the tight feeling in my chest, I let your hand shake while spooning sticky rice onto the porcelain plate, a wedding gift from my grandparents. Forcing a tight-lipped smile, the kind where my eyes winced at the same time, I took my seat in the dining room with Sarah and Wim. We waited for you to join us before eating.

To sit for even a few seconds without racing somewhere was a luxury. I felt exhausted. Supercharged. Even when the twins napped and I crept beside you on the couch, it was hard to simply be, hard to unwind. My brain was always fired up with worry. I couldn't write. I couldn't knit. I couldn't read or scavenge new freelance clients (the old ones had pretty much dried up.) All these things that had once sustained me were far too cerebral now that you were in fact dying. What was the point?

You appeared to be moving in slow motion, concentrating hard while putting food on your plate. I raised my glass to toast Sarah and Wim, and being together. "To good friends."

Had I even taken a sip of wine before my eye caught you tumbling backwards, your body crashing against the black chair as you fell with a thunderous noise onto our floor?

"Brett," I screamed, jumping up. Wim got to you first, reaching behind your body to prop you up. Your mouth was open. You were unconscious. One hundred ninety-seven pounds of dead weight in Wim's arms.

What happened next is a blur to me—your life drained in that moment, and I have no recollection of how long I stood watching you out cold against Wim's body. A minute? Two? Five? It was not the first time I felt dissociated, as though only half of me could process the image of you possibly dead on our floor, but the other half remained frozen, locked in my own vise of seizure. Sarah touched my arm, pulling me back to reality.

I grabbed the blue hospice folder in the kitchen drawer with instructions on who to call in the event of just such an emergency.

"My husband's had a seizure," I said to the 911 operator, my voice fast and abrupt. Sarah put a hand on my back to steady me.

"Please hurry. We live at 309 West 104th Street, Apartment 4C."

I Must Have Packed a Bag for You

YOU REGAINED CONSCIOUSNESS WHILE I WAS still on the phone with 911. You opened your eyes wide, looking like an animal that had narrowly escaped a brush with a predator. I'm sure I asked you if you were all right, but I can't remember any more of the exchange. Wim helped you off the floor and onto the tall black chair you knocked down. It was a lucky thing you didn't hit your head against the edge of the granite countertop.

I have no memory of packing a duffel bag of your clothes—sweatpants, T-shirts, pajamas. When the paramedics came, you didn't want to leave. "I'm fine now," you insisted. I wonder if some part of you knew that this episode would spell the end of life as you knew it, your life at home, with your wife and toddler twins.

It's miraculous to me that Casey and Rebecca slept through the commotion (although anyone living in New York City learns to muffle the noise). Sarah and I rode in the ambulance with you; Wim stayed behind with the sleeping twins until our friend and neighbor Katherine came to relieve him.

The paramedics chattered all along that eerie ride down the FDR Drive. My sphere of reality shifted so that I felt strangely disconnected from you. *Okay, God, what sort of deal can we strike? I'm not ready to lose him yet. Give us more time, please.* It was late, maybe 10:00 p.m. I clutched my winter coat, looking at the city lights out the ambulance window. They danced a blur of blue and red upon the East River. The siren blared. You, next to me, still alive, but leaving me. Sarah, walled off in the front seat, lost in her own private worry. It was deafening.

Arriving at Cabrini Hospice jolted my senses. The fluorescent lights hurt my eyes, and there was too much bustle by the attending staff. I didn't want a warm greeting, I just wanted to get you stable and return home, together. They wheeled you to a small private room with a single bed, red vinyl chair, television, and closet. There were no personal accents, nor was there a memorable view from the window, only roof-tops and water heaters. A nurse changed you into a blue hospital gown, and you lay still and pensive on the tight, white bed. Sarah sat on the visitor's chair. I began to unpack your duffel bag while we waited for your oncologist to meet us. I picked up the jeans you'd been wearing at home and realized as I pulled them away from my face that you'd peed in them. "I'll take these home to wash," I said, avoiding your eyes. "I didn't pee in them," you told me, becoming agitated. "You're making that up." For a man of such reserve and pride, this was the ultimate embarrassment. Sarah looked away, shrinking into the chair. I knew better than to argue. Just then, Dr. Gardner entered the room, rescuing you from your indignity.

"Are you causing trouble?" she teased, to which you smiled. Briefly, she examined your eyes, tested your reflexes, and assessed your neurological functioning.

Later, she would tell me how honored she was to escort you downstairs after chemo treatments, hailing a taxi for you to go to work. You'd stand on the sidewalk with your cane and she'd step into the street outside the clinic at Thirty-eighth Street and First Avenue, raising her white-doctor-coat arm to flag any willing driver in a yellow car. She'd make a gentle fuss about you working on chemo days, but unless your blood counts were dangerously low, you insisted, so the compromise was to put you safely in the cab.

Those were better days. Cabrini Hospice was a place beyond preventive care, hospital clinics, or emergency rooms. Dr. Gardner motioned for me to follow her outside the room to talk. Sarah stayed with you.

Leaning against the manila corridor wall, she asked me about your seizure. She was dressed in a winter parka, not her doctor attire, since it was after hours and she lived within walking distance of Cabrini. "You know he's going to get worse," she told me, one hand stroking her chin, the tone of her voice quiet but commanding. "It was lucky the twins were sleeping."

"Yes, it was lucky," I said, massaging my right eyeball back into focus. "It was horrible to see him like that."

Pause.

"You understand he can't come home now," Dr. Gardner said softly, her eyes locking with mine to silence any resistance.

It struck me that she wasn't asking me what I wished; she was laying out the plain truth. "You won't be able to manage his care much longer, even with home hospice. A seizure like this in front of the children would traumatize them. He'll get much sicker. He needs a different level of care now."

Pause.

"This is very hard, I know."

I didn't say anything because I couldn't find the words. Nothing would have felt right, not "Yes, of course, you know best," or "No, I want him home for as long as possible." I had no idea what "as long as possible" even meant. There was betrayal either way. Leaving you at Cabrini meant defeat; we would have no choice but to wait for your death. Taking you home, well, I knew as a mother that it wasn't right, it wasn't fair, not to the children and not to me. I pressed my cold fingers into balls so tight that my skin turned white around the knuckles. *What would you want? What should I do?* I was still in the hallway and you were still in the room, but the answer came to me clear: *protect the twins.* It was the only truth I needed.

Yes, you helped me make the decision, whether you knew it or not. It was just another way you showed your love for me and the children, a brave parting gift.

"Okay," I said to Dr. Gardner, holding her gaze.

"I'll make arrangements to move him to Calvary in the Bronx." Cabrini offered only short-term hospice care, and not even she could say how long you would last. Days? Weeks?

Bargaining with time, anticipating and prolonging the days, was meaningless. You would remain at Calvary for however long you had to live.

It Was Only Yesterday

IT WAS ONLY YESTERDAY, IT SEEMED, THAT YOUR wavy chestnut hair dipped over your eyebrows, that your green eyes lit when you told a joke, that your olive skin bronzed when you smiled. It was only yesterday, it seemed, that you ate cinnamon rolls for breakfast from the cart by your midtown office. When your pants grew snug around the waist, you laughed about it. "Looks like I'll be working out more," you teased, with a glint of mischief in your eye as you hung yet another dress shirt from the elliptical machine in our bedroom, its finest purpose. *What good problems to have.*

A Place for Us

CALVARY HOSPITAL. Bronx, New York. February 2004.

A crammed parking lot, a lobby full of people with stories. Sky-blue hallways, rooms in salmon, green, or yellow, half-dead plants, shiny linoleum floors. A medical director named Dr. Comfort. Bleak cheer.

Room 440.

A place for the dying. A place for us.

Your Delirium Was Merciful

THE INSIDE OF YOUR HEAD MUST HAVE LOOKED like a mess of electrical wires too frayed and jumbled to function. You had delirium—a medical condition that produces severe confusion in the brain—and it was a blessing. Delirium meant that you had no real sense of being at Calvary, a kind of grace as opposed to knowing you would never return home and had only days to live. "Do you like what we've done to the living room?" you asked colleagues who came to see you a week after you arrived.

For all your bewilderment, though, your peers coming to see you must have registered on a very human level. Thirty of them swooped in one morning in a parade of town cars from Manhattan. You tapped into scarce reserves of physical and mental energy to dress and be wheeled into the common area down the hall for visiting family and friends. It didn't surprise me that you rallied the way you did; you were deeply hurt that no one had sent e-mails or called when you'd finally gone on disability in December, and that no one had visited. As if you had vanished. We couldn't understand it... until I learned by sheer chance after bumping into your old Time Warner colleague Dan Okrent that none of your peers at *Business Week* was aware of the seriousness of your condition. Dan made an inquiry, and it turned out no one knew you were at a hospice, the end near.

Such a serious omission would be stunning to me for years

(a blatant example, I thought, of not understanding the etiquette of illness). But no sooner did the word leak than my phone began to ring, the apologies came, and the colleagues, yes, they came in a show of force so that you would know they cared. It was a remarkable moment to observe you enthroned in your wheelchair in the center of the dayroom with your Olympics cap on, accepting handshakes and soft shoulder rubs. "We miss you, man," a few of them said. "It's not the same without you, Brett." Your words were slurry and unrecognizable, but it hardly mattered, because what you couldn't express you still absorbed. I could see the validation on your face from where I sat across the room, leaving you to bask in this working world of yours one last time. Your colleagues were late in coming, but they came, and you were awake and conscious enough to feel their presence.

Their visit depleted you, I'm sure. Because you never left your bed afterward. From then on, you became even more addled, sleeping heavily.

The next day two top executives from *Business Week* came to your bedside in what would be a somber and uncomfortable goodbye. You could barely keep your eyes open because you were starting to slip into a coma. One of the executives spoke very gently, obviously wanting you to die with a clear head. I would later learn that his sister-in-law had died of a brain tumor years earlier. "You've done a marvelous job, Brett," he told you, leaning in close to your face so that you could register what he was saying. The other executive sat away from the bed, silent and stoic and fidgety. He couldn't wait to leave the room.

Slipping Beyond the Veil of Life

LYING ON THE BED IN YOUR PALE PAJAMAS, YOUR
bald skull and skin green against the white sheets, you appeared to
be shrinking. The more placidly and motionlessly you slept, the more
diminutive you became to me. When I sat quietly on the beige chair
at the foot of your bed, it was almost as if I had entered a dream state,
watching you slowly evaporate.

It occurred to me in such moments that I was willing you to die.
Beyond regret, I wanted it to be over, your suffering, our suffering.
That I could make you disappear in my mind prepared me for the
inevitable moment when you would return to dust. Hands clasped
in prayer under my chin, I sat on that chair, waiting for you to take
your last breath (*would it be today?*) with only a clock above my head
to remind me of real time.

Images like Gold

THE ANGST OF MY VIGIL WAS TEMPERED WHEN I
brought Casey and Rebecca to visit. Full of toddler energy, they infused
the hospice floor with life. In and out of your room they would prance,
giggling as they touched the nurses' circular station and pranced back
again. "I see you," they teased. To them, you had always been sick.
Which is not to say they didn't feel grief.

I have an enduring image of the twins lying against you on the
bed soon after you'd arrived at Calvary (but before the herd came
from *Business Week*). Casey is wearing an ivory turtleneck with
dancing animals and your blue cap. Our son's bottom is rooted to
the mattress, but his torso appears pitched forward, the tension of
the moment manifest. Rebecca, dressed in a jean overall dress, is shy,
burying herself in the limp flesh of your arm. You summon the strength
to hold them steady. You aren't smiling. Your mouth is cracked and
white at the corners. You are struggling. Quickly, I take the photograph
and remove the twins from the bed. That image and a few others
taken of the four of us seconds earlier are our last as a family.

Too painful to appreciate in present time, someday, the social
worker and psychologists told me, these images will be like gold to
the children. They were right. The twins will not remember visiting
you at Calvary, or even saying their final goodbyes on the day you
died. Years later they will ask, repeatedly, "Why couldn't we meet

him?" Or "What did he look like when he died?" Then, on each birthday, or at the start of the new school year, or in the darkness of their pastel rooms just before sleep, they will ask, "Why did Daddy have to die?"

We Made a Nervous Vigil

ON YOUR TENTH DAY AT CALVARY, THE ONSET of your coma was unmistakable. When you weren't sleeping, you were so groggy that your head tipped and your eyelids shut. You seemed unaware of my presence, your parents' presence. I couldn't imagine the grief your parents felt at losing you, their first child. Your mom would not crack for fear she would break. She was always put together, her makeup set, dressed (defiantly, I thought) in bold colors, her hair spray and perfume creating a clean waft. Your dad was far less veiled; he drew inward, shoulders slumped, wishing he could trade places with you.

We made a nervous vigil: Mom making small talk about the children, kind as always ("How did they sleep?" she asked, not knowing what else to say); Dad clearing the phlegm in his throat loudly while pacing the room and hall ("Achem, achem, achem," he sounded); I, with cold, clammy fingers, tight chest, wired. I remember wanting to devour food, wanting especially to suck down a Burger King Whopper or two. I was maniacally hungry all the time. I'd sit beside you while you slept, munching without any thought to what I was putting into my own body, which was little more than a vessel to contain such titanic feelings of sadness. I neither gained nor lost weight during this time; the food held me, stopping time as it tethered me to you. You couldn't chew anything solid, so possibly I ate for the two of us, I don't know.

When I think about this day—day ten—and the hours building to your death, I can still hear the sound of your snoring, so jarring, discordant, unnatural. Occasionally you startled yourself awake, thrusting your body as if in a paroxysm. And then you would moan, your anxiety palpable. You opened your eyes, and your mother and I rushed to your side, offering chocolate pudding and sips of water. "Take a drink, honey," I'd say, propping the straw close to your mouth. "Please, darling, have something," your mom begged. We resisted seeing that it was too late for pudding and water, too late for any earthly nourishment. You couldn't speak or swallow. From now on, you would taste only crushed ice brushed against your lips. From now on, you would be fed only intravenous medicines to lessen your seizures, pain, and fear.

"He's slipping now," one of the nurses said in a frank voice. She had observed your mom and me trying to feed you. "I can get the doctor if you like."

It was absurd, I know, to cling to life when death felt so near, yet you were still alive sleeping on the bed, so shouldn't we do all we could for you?

I wanted more time.

It Took Twelve Days

THE AIR IN NEW YORK CITY WAS CHILLY THAT morning, February 21. At 6:30 a.m., the sky looked pale, almost colorless. Sipping my coffee while driving a half hour north toward Calvary, I felt a softness that I hadn't in days. It was good to notice a world beyond the hospice—high buildings, cars, traffic lights, sparse city trees, dense clouds, and National Public Radio playing. Paying attention to these sights and sounds calmed me even if it held a certain irony that you could die within hours. You were deep in a coma; there was no telling how long you would last.

I was at your bedside shortly before 7:00 a.m. My parents had the twins in Connecticut. I kissed your forehead like always, but you didn't stir. The morning light made a shadow across the chair, and I sat for a moment, basking in its yellow warmth. I didn't detect any changes in you from the previous night. You looked serene, like a vision in white—real, but surreal, too. How is it that from your head up you were so sick when from your chest down you appeared healthy, normal? Your body showed no signs of disease beyond the pastiness of your flesh. At six foot one, you were still tall, even in bed, and you were still a decent weight. Had you been able to trade heads, you might have walked away a man reborn.

The peace of the morning was short-lived because your breath began to fail you. It had been happening all along, of course, but something urgent had shifted for you. You started to gasp and suck the air, making pained, garbled sounds that could only have risen from the depth of your torment. Your parents and sister could hear you from the hallway. Your mouth was agape, and every so often you startled, causing your eyes, which were closed, to flutter as if wind-blown. I worried you might be afraid. "Does he know that he's in a coma?" I asked one of the nurses. Your family and I gathered by your side. "No, he's not aware," she reassured us, noting that your blood pressure was dropping. "I'm going to alert the doctor. His breathing will become more labored now."

Which it did, almost on cue; you started to choke on the air. You couldn't inhale, couldn't exhale. We stood by your bed, horrified to watch the jerking rise and fall of your chest. You were still fighting to live, your breath, the bridge, buckling.

At some point that morning, my parents brought the twins to say goodbye. Had I not written it down, I wouldn't remember that Casey climbed atop your unconscious body, kissing you on the cheek as he squirmed, and said, "Bye, Daddy." Rebecca was frightened; I held her close to you, but she would not leave my arms. You on your deathbed was too much for them to process—not that they were capable of distinguishing unconscious from dead. *They were too young to under-stand the importance of saying goodbye, too young for the sort of closure words can create. Although they have no memory of that last visit, at least I can honestly meet their searching eyes and say, "Yes, you said goodbye. Here is how it happened."*

The rushed parting was necessary; my parents took a moment with you, thanking you for being such a good son-in-law as they held your lifeless hand. My mother was trying hard not to erupt into hysteria in front of the twins. My dad was equally broken up, yet his emotions were trapped inside his body. They took the twins back to Connecticut to wait. I promised that I would call them once you had passed.

When it was over, we would have the whole of our lives to mourn you.

Chorus of Angels

I DON'T REMEMBER ALL THE TINY MOMENTS OF that day, or how it came to be that a crowd of seventeen shared your death. Had I known this would be your last day, I would have kindly asked the visitors, who came in force and mostly unscheduled, to leave. They straggled in that morning before and during the twins' visit, and throughout the afternoon.

Who had written this script? My friend Rachel, Uncle Harvey, Aunt Ilene, cousins Seth and Josetta, all from California; cousins Jon, Phil, Linda, Joel, and Adam; your best friend, George; my brother, Greg. Friends of your parents. Beyond the family from California, it's not as though we'd sounded the alarm that you would die within hours; people just showed up. There was so much commotion, everyone literally rubbing against one another in the small room to see and touch you before you died, to hug us, your family, and say heartfelt things like "I'm so sorry" and "We are here for you." In and out of your room they came, needing to say goodbye although never imagining you would actually die in their company. When they understood that they were in fact trespassing upon your final minutes, they rooted themselves to the room. Some stronger urge must have prevailed, because no one thought to ask, "Is it okay if we stay?"

At the time, it felt wrong, the idea of all these people witnessing such an intimate moment. And yet I couldn't have sent them away if

I'd tried. The love for you, for us, was overpowering. I sat down on the pillow beside your head and tuned them out.

"He'll last another hour at most," Dr. Pappous explained gently as he took your pulse, now faint. He wasn't much older than you, probably in his mid-forties, and a father of young children himself. He put his hand on my shoulder for support. This doctor who ushered the living into the land of death had been so kind to you and our family. "Thank you, Doctor," your father said. "Thank you for all you've done." Dr. Pappous didn't respond. What was there to say?

Now, your breath, when you managed to take one, was hard and unexpected. I cradled your head and upper body in my arms, trying to calm your fitful movements. In spite of your dead weight, you were so lost to me that you might have slipped through my fingers like a ghost. I was lost to myself at this moment, too, dissociated even from the weight of my body against yours. "Shhhh," I whispered. "It's okay now."

Still, you fought.

Each time I tried to soothe you, you seemed to gasp for more air. As if you wanted to say, "I'm not leaving yet."

But you were leaving me.

"Shhhh," I continued. "You're all right now." I stroked the back of your head while pressing my damp cheek against your face. Your breath smelled sour.

"Let go," said your cousin Seth.

"It's okay, Brettski," said your cousin Jon.

"Let go, let go," said the crowd around me in soft voices. They circled us like a halo, the force of their gentle chant building. "Let go," they sang. Your parents and sister sat on the middle and end of the bed by your feet and arms, gripping their last hold on you. I was aware of feeling very hot, the heat of our collective grief. "Let go. Let go. Let go," went the crowd, their love lifting us all. "Let go," they continued, in harmony, faceless now. My eyes, all our eyes, fixed on you.

The room quieted. "It's okay," I whispered in your ear. You stirred slightly (or was it just my imagination?) but made no more sounds. I nudged myself closer. "Let go, let go," the chorus of angels began again, softer now. "Let go."

We kept on this way—the crowd, me, you—until we drowned out the last of your uneven breaths with the steady rhythm of our voices. "Let go," we said one final time.

You died in my arms at 4:45 p.m. Dr. Pappous announced your death.

Some time passed, I can't say how long, but when I looked up from the bed I thought I saw a shaft of window light fall upon the room.

A Mystery

IT'S A MYSTERY, LOVE AND DEATH AND FAITH
and the way God, I think, works. I wouldn't have planned your death
that way, surrounded by people. I would have asked to be alone with
you. I would have asked that the doctor and nurses and your family
wait outside the door. The twins would have already kissed you
goodbye, saying, "We'll see you another time." Then I would have
stretched out beside you on the bed with my head on your shoulder,
the way I always did. Those warm husband shoulders would comfort
me still, just as my head near yours would seal us together. "You'll
always be with me," I would have told you. And the part of you that
still lived (your soul?) would have understood this truth.

There is no order, no rationale for such matters. Some benign
force must have intervened, because you would not have wanted me
to witness your death alone.

Grace, it must have been.

PART THREE

Both Sides

We Go Where We Need to Go

WHEN AT LAST BRETT DIED, I EXPECTED PEACE, not chaos all over again. Maybe it was naïve of me, but he was sick for so long—dying for the majority of our marriage, nearly seven of our eleven years together. Again and again I buried him prematurely even as I wanted him to prove everyone wrong and live. For as much as I wanted the suffering to end, the false hopes to stop, the part of me that could stare beyond fear prayed for a miracle. The tension of his illness drained me dry. In calm moments, too, those periods beyond crises and treatments, if I stilled my heart, I could almost see him disappear, bodily flesh and spirit at once.

Now that Brett really was gone, part of me thought his death would be easier. It's only because he was sick for so many years that I expected to feel some release afterward. I wished that had been the case. So many times during his illness, people outside of our inner world would ask, "How do you do it?" By which they meant how do I continue living, year after year, with a man who would surely die. The askers meant no malice, but innocent and supportive as the questions purported to be, they stunned me. *Did I have a choice? I wouldn't have dreamt of leaving.*

Right away everyone wants the widow to hurt less. Right away everyone tries to lift her. The Manual of Mourning must be out of print because I was not immediately ready to receive the good intentions of others. They wanted to heal me, I wanted to heal me, but I was mistaken about the time this process would actually require, in spite of having anticipated Brett's death. You simply can't remove the bridge between life, death, and life again in a matter of weeks. I didn't understand that the fear I fought when Brett was alive would morph into other fears—from practical matters, which ballooned to a size disproportionate to my ability to address them clearly, to my own sanity. These fears shook and paralyzed me so that sometimes it was hard to recognize myself.

I wish I could have placed an arm around my thirty-seven-year-old self and said, "The veil of sadness will lift. The death will linger for a time, but you will endure it. For now, go where you need to go."

Child and Wife and Mother at Once

WE NEVER DISCUSSED CEMETERY PLOTS. The idea was too morbid and real, as ridiculous as that sounds given the ample time we had to prepare for Brett's death. I really can't imagine having spoken to him about the matter; I don't think I could have held his gaze.

The detail would not go unnoticed, however, as my father-in-law, Stan, a consummate planner, had it all sorted out in his head. Just hours after Brett died, while sitting on the rug in the twins' room, a bourbon in his shaking hand, he blurts out, "We'd really like for Brett to be buried near us, in Long Island." He doesn't give me time to respond because he so wants this issue to be resolved quickly. "You will have a life, you will marry again. Please."

It's the pleading tone in his voice that momentarily takes me out of my pain and into his. His shoulders are slumped, giving him a sunken look. His skin looks sunken, too; it's ash gray, the color of misery. He has lost his oldest child, his only son. The deal he made with God about trading places with Brett failed. "Please," he says a second time.

There isn't a chance on earth I'd say no. Not only because I love my in-laws and haven't thought this far ahead—to burial plots and headstones—but also because I realize in this rare and primal expression of a father's need that I am more than Brett's wife: I am also Ron and Sue's daughter, Stan and Brenda's daughter-in-law, and the mother of their grandchildren. The most horrible image surfaces in my brain. *What if it were my son?* Yes, I would want him next to me. Stone to stone. When you die young, this is a parent's right.

This Deep Ravine or That Jagged Cliff?

WE NEVER TALKED ABOUT HIS FUNERAL EITHER, what he wanted in terms of a service, who would speak, where, or even if he wanted to be physically buried.

Imagine.

We entrusted our financial affairs to a planner, a kind woman who was referred to us by my social worker at CancerCare. Up until the last year of Brett's life, he'd handled the business aspects of the marriage: the bills, college fund, savings, car. Gender-stereotyped as it might have been for a contemporary couple, I never had any interest in these things because I didn't have to. He was proud to take care of them, and I was happy and busy enough with work and motherhood to let him.

He hated to let go of this responsibility. "I can do it," he'd say. "Come let me show you." For reasons that embarrass me now for their childishness, I zoned out whenever he tried to share monthly statements from Charles Schwab or Fidelity. It's easy, he seemed to suggest as he breezed through page after page of reports that looked like identical muck to me. "I just don't get it," I'd tell him, making some lame excuse that I needed to check on one of the twins, start a load of wash, or empty the dishwasher. I would have mopped the building's pockmarked lobby floor and shined its old brass elevator if it meant not having to absorb the weight of all this financial matter, the tipping point in the tower of responsibility that was crushing me months before his actual death. I wanted to delegate the job to someone else—the financial planner—so that I didn't have to worry about Yet Another Thing. We never argued about the issue; Brett consented to outside help when he was coherent enough to put me at ease.

One groggy morning when he was still at home and the hospice aide was in the living room stacking and knocking down Tupperware with the twins, he told me that he hoped I would remarry someday. He lay in his wrinkled undershirt, his head sideways on the pillow, heavy-lidded eyes on mine. My head rested on the other pillow as I took the words in. I didn't say anything.

"I mean it," he said.

Tears filled my eyes, and I pressed my body against his and we held each other close, without words.

So it isn't as though we didn't speak about life after his death. We just would not talk about the death itself, beginning with where he would like to die—the apartment or hospital? As if it was an agreeable choice, like jump into this deep ravine or off that jagged cliff. The truth is that neither one of us wanted to go there, even as the end hovered.

What is clear to me only now, eight years later, is that I spared Brett's feelings in order to protect him from further hurt. He would have done the same for me; it was how we loved each other against a mountain of doom. Such politeness might have created a quiet distance between us, but it was respectful and, in its own way, pure.

A Funeral Befitting a Good Man

VISIONS OF BRETT'S FUNERAL TAUNTED ME through his long illness: ivory gladiolas, mustached men in navy suits, distraught women holding white handkerchiefs, and a procession of dark, cherrywood caskets, enough for all the times I imagined he died.

Such dreams, phantasmagoric as they were, served a higher purpose now that Brett was dead: plans fell into place with surprising ease. The venue was obvious—it would have to be on the Upper West Side, the place we called home for fifteen years. I never looked beyond the Riverside Memorial Chapel on West Seventy-sixth Street.

There was no question either that I would involve Cantor Gilbert, the childhood cantor who had performed Brett's Bar Mitzvah and my Bat Mitzvah when we were thirteen, and who'd married us in 1993. At my urging, he came to talk to Brett at Calvary about connecting with his spiritual center. Like particles of dust, the words dissipated into the heavy air around him. To me, it didn't matter that the message was lost. Peace, however possible, that was all I wanted him to feel.

Erik Kolbell, the wise friend we'd relied on during so many crisis moments, would certainly speak. He was, after all, a minister and psychologist. And at some point, Dr. Balmaceda, Brett's first oncologist, asked if she could say a few words, a gesture that touched me deeply. She felt close to us, confiding many times about her children and deteriorating marriage. Often she read my fears and made herself available by phone or in person. She called and visited even when Brett was no longer her patient.

I could have asked a dozen people to speak on behalf of Brett's professional life. But I chose Dan Okrent. Brett had a lot of respect for Dan. "He's so smart," he used to tell me with a mixture of pride and yearning. Beyond their days together at Time Inc., Brett kept his eye on Dan, watching him become the first public editor of *The New York Times* in 2003.

And I spoke. *How could I not?*

What Was Said

FEATHER CANYONS EVERYWHERE, THE SONG "BOTH
Sides Now" echoed in the exalted space, one last time for Brett.

From Erik Kolbell: A young man who had not an enemy on earth,
who was the genuine article in a world full of frauds, a man who was
so consumed with the idea that his family needed to be provided for
that he worked to the very last day he was conscious, a young man
of unbridled promise and unquestioned integrity up and dies on us
before his race is halfway done.

We drop sticks in the sand, we make an overture. We insinuate
ourselves into the life of another in some way so small as to be barely
perceptible. A little jog in a gentle current. We see how any gesture,
however small, can change the direction of whole lives.

Brett was a man of small gestures with great meaning, because I do
not believe he made them carelessly. I believe there was intention behind
every time Brett dropped by a colleague's office, intention behind every
nod or smile to strangers and friends, a world of intention behind
his dream that Nancy would one day be his wife, that Casey and
Rebecca would be his enduring legacy.

A time to work and a time to rest. It is not ours to say when, or
why. What we *can* do, in the face of all times, trials, and triumphs, is
love one another. Be exceedingly, generously, recklessly kind to one
another. Let us do this for Brett.

From Daniel Okrent: Anyone who worked with Brett knew that *work* was a term that really didn't apply for him. His office life was continuous with his home life—not in the sense of the driven executive who can't turn off his engine at the end of the day, but in the sense of someone whose existence was fully integrated, his sense of himself fully comfortable. The privilege was all ours.

From Dr. Balmaceda: She spoke movingly, but I just can't remember what she said.

From me: Brett's strength of character, dignity, and brave spirit will enrich my world, and our children's lives, always. At last, Brett, you can stop fighting and be at peace... Let us sit together in a moment of quiet grace, for Brett.

"Amazing Grace." *How sweet the sound.*

Not a dry eye as the song played.

A Whirl of People, So Much Food

WHEN JEWISH PEOPLE GRIEVE, THEY EAT.
My closest college friends, most of them Jewish as it happens, saw to it that anyone who wanted to come by our apartment after the funeral would be fed. The girls ordered trays of whitefish salad, herring, smoked salmon, tomatoes, capers, and onions. There were bagels, rugelach, and babka. All from Zabar's, a New York bastion of sensory overload. The smell of the food, salty and sweet at once, fused with the earthy aroma of brewed coffee, filled our apartment, a gentle reminder that life ought to be tasted.

I wish I could recall who else sent baskets of food, but I'm sure they do. It was all appreciated and eaten.

So many people made shivah calls those first few days. Shivah is the official period of mourning in the Jewish tradition, although ours lasted three, not seven days. Hosting a houseful of people for a week after losing Brett was more than I could handle, and too overstimulating for the twins. I remember being boxed into our skinny hallway at one point that first afternoon, looking without really seeing the crowd in our home. People were everywhere—on the couches, on the rose rug, in the foyer, at the dining room table, by the elevator—talking, eating, talking more. I haven't a clue what they were saying. There was so much commotion, the volume high and steady. Nowhere to hide, not even our bedroom, since our bed—no, *my* bed now—was piled high with coats.

Over five hundred people attended the morning service. Who among them was at our house now? I cannot recall a single conversation, a single hug, a single bite of bagel and lox. I have a faint image of sitting on one of the kitchen stools with Erik Kolbell; my brother, Greg; my sister-in-law, Marcy; and my college friends, but it was late at night and the crowds had already gone. My parents and Brett's parents, too, had returned to Connecticut, where they would begin their own shivah the next day.

Someone must have helped me put the twins to bed. They were wired from the energy in the house, too young to understand that death was not like a game of hide-and-seek, that no matter how hard they searched for their father, he could not be found. There would be no "peekaboo, I see you." For now, the children had a house full of playmates who distracted them with real black-and-white cookies at their toy kitchen.

All these memories of love in our home and the false high we felt those first days are blurry. But I remember the salmon and chocolate babka.

Anesthesia

BEYOND NORMAL EXHAUSTION, THE WIDOW'S
fatigue is like an acute numbness and distortion of life. Nothing is as
it was before. The lights in the hallway flicker and glare, causing your
eyes to shudder; the area rug shifts beneath your feet; and the black
couch, once a haven of comfort, no longer supports you. You see
large objects only, like the refrigerator, which is so cluttered it wants
to scream "enough" each time you smash another tub of cream cheese
(that someone has kindly brought) onto a shelf. Gluttony at a time like
this? it asks. In these raw moments of grief your eyes play tricks on
you because you see only the broadest of shapes; life lacks definition.

Ordinary sounds hurt. The phone and flush of the toilet irritate and
doors close with a bang, but worst of all is that the children's voices
are more squawk than chord. You cannot bear to hear them cry.
Or laugh. Or play. They are only thirty-three months old, toddlers
who are supposed to be active, children who are supposed to be
seen and heard. It kills you that you feel this way—an unfit mother,
you think—but at the moment it's completely true. Some days the
disillusionment gets so bad that you ask your mother to take the
twins. "Mom. Please. Help," you ask meekly like a child. She and
my dad feel awful, and of course, they help. Everyone helps. You
don't really want your parents or in-laws or brother or sister-in-law
to permanently take the twins, nothing like that; it's just that you feel

too numb and lifeless to parent right now.

Your brain is like a bag of frozen peas that has burst open. The peas, which are your thoughts, scatter like loose pellets and jangle your insides. Your body stiffens from these mini glaciers that render you temporarily immobile. You really can't seem to move. For a moment you wonder if this is the same bag of peas you used to nurse your crotch three years ago, before the twins, before Brett's cancer returned to finish him off. You think you might be going crazy.

It would be months before I could bring myself to read the widow literature, and when I did, one line sailed above the others for its reverberating power.

Grief carries its own anesthesia, Lady Bird Johnson told *Time* magazine a few months after her husband, President Lyndon Johnson, died in 1973. He had only recently left office.

Yes, that's right. Grief is its own anesthesia. You lose a loved one and you lose all sensation.

Mommy Always Comes Back

HERE IS WHAT I TOLD MY CHILDREN IN THE WAKE
of their father's death: Mommy always comes back.

The words became a temporary lifeline those first few months, the children hanging on them like leaves on a tree. Every time I took them to preschool or left them with Eurita, our sitter, to make a supermarket run, there were equal amounts of tears, wails, and tugging at my knees. "Mama, don't go. Don't go."

Eurita, bless her, was strong enough to scoop them up in both arms and lull them with her gentle Caribbean voice. "Hush now, it's okay. Mommy will be back." More tears. "Casey! Rebecca! Hush now, Mommy will be back!" She bounced them playfully on her hips, chanting "Woops and woops and woops," and they had no choice but to squeal. Which was my cue to leave.

"I love you, I love you," I'd sing, running out the door to make a clean exit, feeling guilty and free at the same time.

And When Mommy Came Back

NAKED JOY. That is what it felt like to walk into the apartment
and hear my children scream "Mama," running toward me as if the
world was born again. They would grab at my thighs, wanting to be
picked up, and for a moment—as long as I could hold them close
against my chest—we stayed in a pure embrace. Such greetings were
stripped bare, free from all burden: nothing more than a mother and
her children loving fully, drawing nourishment from the cup of life.

Fits and starts. That's how Casey and Rebecca dealt with Brett's
death. One minute they were playing happily on the living room rug,
moments later their sunny moods darkened and they became clingy
and frightened. They needed to know my whereabouts at all times,
and this I understood. Losing their father cracked open their sense
of safety in the world. Some days the whining never seemed to end,
and it took massive restraining on my part not to lock myself in the
bedroom and throw my own tantrum. We were all entitled to pitch
fits, yet someone, me, had to be in control.

In so many ways, Casey and Rebecca were still babies. Apart
from the occasional mimicking "Mommy always comes back" or
"Daddy is in our hearts," they lacked the ability to put words to their
feelings. For the most part, they expressed their grief physically.
Rebecca yanked so much hair from her delicate head that she left
a bald spot. Strand by fine strand, as if she was trying to pluck her

fears, exposing the very nakedness she was feeling. The hair pulling had begun before Brett died but was far worse now.

Casey was wild with energy, with no one place, no one thing ever seizing his focus: restlessness that was hard to soothe. He walked on his toes, one of many sensory-seeking habits that grief intensifies. This I would learn from our social worker, Jill, whom I relied on heavily in the time after Brett's death to help me navigate the emotional minefield we now inhabited.

Jill helped me find the right language to talk to the twins. Without her, I would have spared their feelings, as I had done with Brett. Left on my own, I'm sure that I would have veered away from all talk of cancer and illness and hospitals and Daddy and death, not wanting to cause them more pain. In the interest of protecting Rebecca and Casey from further hurt, I would have done the exact opposite of what Jill counseled. Retelling what had happened and labeling their feelings, no matter how difficult it was for me, or uncomfortable for them, was exactly how I needed to support them.

"Children want facts," Jill explained.

She sketched simple booklets with plainspoken language: "Daddy was so sick that he died. He didn't want to die, and nobody else wanted him to die. But sometimes doctors can't help people stay alive when they are very, very sick. When Daddy died his body stopped working. He couldn't move anymore or talk or eat or see or hear." The twins would look at Jill's face as she read to them, or hop on my lap, transfixed by the words and line drawings of their daddy lying still on the hospital bed. She told them about the special box he was buried in. "See," she said, pointing to the next page—the coffin on paper.

"What does it mean to be very, very sick?" they wanted to know. Month after month, the same questions. "Can you die of a cold?"

The clean truth. In manageable doses. That was what they deserved.

"Yes, Mommy is sad because she misses Daddy," I'd tell them. "And when Mommy is sad she sometimes cries." No child likes to see her mother cry, but for my children, stable ground shifted. Panic spread across their faces and they rushed at me with all the force their tiny bodies contained. "Don't cry. Don't cry." Which made *them* cry, hard. I remember these moments not because I cried often, but because I cried very little around them. Those peas had not yet defrosted.

Little Man, Big Man

"DON'T WORRY, MAMA," CASEY SAID TO ME THE morning after Brett died. "I'll find my daddy and bring him home to you." We were sitting on the black stools at the kitchen island.

I spilled my coffee.

Little did I know how much responsibility my young son felt for restoring our family, or the way he instinctively wanted to protect his sister and me. Little did I know that he felt it was "his job" to take care of me, as though he had graduated overnight to man of the house in his father's absence.

Casey would carry the weight of his father's death for years.

Be five.

Be six.

Be seven.

Be eight.

Be nine.

Be ten.

Year after year, I would have to remind him to be the little boy he still was. "It's my job to take care of you," I'd say. "And I love that job."

No therapy has been able to shake this primal need to be my protector. We still struggle with overnights and camp. "Mom, I don't want to leave you," he'll say. "I need to be around."

A few times: "I'm your husband. And I'm never going to leave you."

"No, no, you are my son."

Little man, big man. It would be his deepest scar.

Where Is Daddy?

THE MYSTERIOUSNESS OF DEATH IS CONFOUNDING enough for adults, but how exactly do you explain gone forever, heaven, spirit, and soul to three-year-olds?

The twins struggled to know their dad's whereabouts. To them, he had to be somewhere and that somewhere was a concrete place.

I didn't bring them to the funeral; they were too young and our family was too distraught. Nor had I taken them to Brett's grave in Long Island since the site would remain a pile of dirt until his parents and I put a headstone there, which according to Jewish custom typically happens a year after the physical death—allowing time for the body to decay and the soul to rise. Not only would the twins not understand this concept, but the idea of Brett lying beneath a mound of dirt would have terrified them.

So one day Jill created "Casey and Rebecca's Cemetery Book." She drew a casket, a headstone, a hole in the ground, and rows of graves, all things tied to place. "Each grave," she explained, "has a special stone or marker on it so that people will know who is buried there." One page shows us standing by Brett's stone. "Rebecca doesn't want to touch the stone because she doesn't want her hands to get dirty. She says she will see when she gets there whether or not she will touch the stone. Rebecca wants Casey to touch the stone. Here is Rebecca watching Casey touch the stone. Rebecca is thinking about if she will touch it."

It makes me laugh to think of this today—how my darling daughter was only concerned about not getting her hands dirty. Grief, after all, is messier than the muddiest trench. In other words: she was already in deep.

"People feel very sad and mad when they visit cemeteries," Jill continued. "They think about how much they miss the people who died and how they wish they could come back. Everyone is sad that Daddy can't come back: Nana, Papa, Aunt Marcy and Uncle Jaime, Gammy and Grandpa, Uncle Greg." In the center of this page, I am seen hugging the twins, and off to the right are Brett's parents, holding hands.

The story ends with as much closure as is realistic. The twins and I are seated on our black couch looking at pictures from our visit to the cemetery, broken but together. The book of loss is not easily stored away.

Fuzzy Thinking

CASEY KEEPS PUTTING ON BRETT'S SHOES AND walking toward the door. "I'm going out to find my daddy," he announces.

Unlike her brother, Rebecca invokes her father in a remembering sort of way. She says, "My daddy likes his bagel warm. My daddy likes coffee."

And then, more abstractly, "The window is sad."

I keep expecting to wake up one morning and find Brett sitting on the large chair, coffee and PalmPilot in hand. Or to bump against him at night. As every widow reports, I do not yet sleep on his side of the bed. That space is his, and it hardly matters that he isn't alive to claim it. I am almost spooked at the idea of shifting positions, even toward the middle of the bed. I stay on the left side, like always.

Spring and Going Places

NOT SURPRISINGLY, I HAD TROUBLE SLEEPING. Even with Klonopin, my thoughts raced. I woke early, 5:00 or 5:30 a.m., bone-tired. I turned thirty-eight that May and wrote, "I am no longer a wife. I am a widow."

I wanted to breathe deep, cleansing breaths all spring, yet each time I exhaled it was as if my gut swelled with flat, stagnant air. What had taken years to accumulate would take years to release.

Rebecca coped similarly with layers of feelings buried inside. It was only at six and seven and eight and nine and ten that her grief emerged, sporadically, and each year with a deeper ability to question. Missing her dad makes her feel incomplete; it is the sort of hurt that never fully leaves.

That first year, however, it was Casey whose upset unraveled me. He still camped outside the bedroom door, waiting for Brett, although gradually this activity began to morph into other "seeking" behavior. He repeated himself, intentionally crashed into objects and people, and fixated on cars, specifically, our black Jetta. "Should I get the car, Mama?" he'd ask with eyes round as yo-yos.

Here is why: he believed that his father would be in the passenger seat. Brett wasn't able to drive the last years of his life, so I pushed the twins in the double stroller to the garage, four short blocks north and three long blocks east, where we kept our car. From there I bundled them into their car seats, and together we drove to pick up Brett at the apartment. It was the same routine whether we went to the doctor's office or hospital or to see our families in Connecticut on weekends.

The image remains vivid. There was Brett standing with one hand around the brass pole of the building's canopy and the other on his cane. In the chill of autumn and winter he wore baggy jeans, his red Patagonia jacket, wool scarf, and a baseball cap to cover his bare head. The building superintendent, a kind man and grandfather named Gilbert, hovered nearby, trying not to crowd Brett but placing himself in close enough proximity to catch him should he stumble. Only once or twice did I ask Gilbert to do this (without telling Brett, who would have been appalled), but Gilbert made himself present when it was time for us to go anywhere.

"Daddy, Daddy," Casey would shout the minute we turned onto 104th Street and he spotted Brett. "Our family!" He bounced in the car seat, legs moving with such enthusiasm I thought he would tear himself free from the tight straps. "Daddy, Daddy," he cried again when I stopped the car and Brett slowly lowered himself onto the seat. "Our family!"

I couldn't have imagined the way our car became a cradle of togetherness. On days when Brett had the strength, he would play a Beatles CD, singing "Hey Jude" to the kids. Forget the stanza about sad songs; they loved only *na na na na, na na na.*

I remember, too, driving along the tree-lined Merritt Parkway toward Connecticut listening to Brett sing "Take Me Out to the Ball Game." By then a part of him must have known that he would never take his son to a ball game. But they would have the song. And the ride in the car.

That Casey would develop an obsession with cars was just another way to hold on to his dad. Daddy was safe in the car. And the car took us places—as a family. Later, Casey left toy cars on his father's gravestone. And a few times, he would ask with three-year-old innocence and heart, "Can I take the car to heaven?"

A Brief Respite

I TOOK MYSELF ON A GRIEF TRIP. My parents and in-laws cared for the twins, which, in spite of their lingering sadness, was healthy for everyone. I went alone to St. Martin, a favorite place of Brett's and mine, a place with nothing but positive memories. St. Martin would comfort me because I could picture us there together. I was not yet looking to prove anything to myself about how I would carry forward as a young widowed woman, or the minute and broad ways I would surprise myself by leaping into new territory—a solitary landscape.

I only wanted to be alone. My mother asked to join me, and I might have called a friend, though the idea of sharing space, feeling accountable, shadowed, having to speak (or not), wanting to cry (or not), needing to rage (or not), felt suffocating. Bloated from the weight of the past few months, I could visualize one thing only: a bright, open place to catch my breath and think.

The uneasy truth is that home overwhelmed me. The ordinary business of life does not pause; the same household jobs you had before multiply. For me as well, even though all along I had been the one buying and changing diapers, preparing meals, giving baths. "You're so capable," friends said, repeatedly. Yes. And no. Because the emotional undertow of widowhood was powerful, more challenging even than the physical demands of parenting toddler twins.

No one predicts how the vat of mourning is exposed when the

husband who has occupied all your caregiving energy for seven years finally dies. How is it that the caregiver managed to juggle everything at once? At fleeting, scattershot moments, drowning becomes tempting, an easy way out. But you can't give up for the very fact that your children need you; their lives depend upon your survival. In spite of the riptide of loss that threatens to knock you unconscious, you understand this privilege (a form of love) in the haziest sense. You must carry forward. You must parent. You must live.

And what of all the "death and dying" paperwork? The widow is thrown a mountain of administrative gobbledygook that must be taken seriously—medical claims, insurance benefits, Social Security papers, title changes to cars and houses, probate documents. On and on the list of Things to Be Taken Care Of spins, with no clear end point. On days when she clings to a sliver of perspective, she has to stop and think, *Who has time to mourn?*

For all the ways I dreaded these new responsibilities, and for all the times I felt sorry for myself, I wondered how much harder the job would be with no family and fewer resources.

St. Martin gave me a momentary respite, a sanctuary to see this new horizon. Being alone felt no less lonely than I already felt on the inside, so somehow it was okay to walk alone, read alone, swim alone, eat alone. Sunshine freckling my arms. Sand in between my toes. The pleasing, parched taste of sea air. Outstretched ocean to look upon with no required focal point.

And silence.

I don't doubt that a few family and friends wondered, *How can she leave the twins at such a time?* No one questioned me, but had anyone voiced concern, this is what I would have said: "I have nothing left to give right now."

Little did I realize at the time, but I was already showing that I could care for the three of us in this altered life. A calmer me meant a calmer, more capable mother.

The Widow's Curse

ST. MARTIN UNVEILED ANOTHER UNEXPECTED
insight—the widow's curse. A fantasy of my own marred imagination that would taunt me like meat on a bone, the widow's curse was
the curse of being seen for what I now was: A WIDOW. I hated the
harsh sound of the words, the damning, separate identity that, from
the moment Brett died, stuck.

Nothing in my life experience warranted such prejudice—wasn't
I, after all, a sophisticated New Yorker? Yet the feeling of being
looked at differently was inescapable. People who knew Brett, those
familiar with our story, family and friends in Connecticut, California, Colorado, Minnesota, and Arizona, would, of course, see
me with new eyes. *Their* empathetic eyes weren't the problem. The
"curse" came from strangers who passed me on the street, mothers
on the tot lot, even acquaintances and firefighters, whom I imagined
read the hurt and strain on my face, peering straight through me to
the source of all brokenness. Didn't they realize I only wanted to
remain invisible?

Narcissistic as it was (and mourning, I came to see, gives gentle
license to such entitlement), I felt transparent from skin to soul.
Nothing could disguise the fragility I mirrored, or the way a black
heaviness hung around me, the word WIDOW smeared across my
forehead like tar.

In the practical sense, this inexplicable shame meant that "I'M WIDOWED" were among the first words I spoke when introducing myself to a vacationing couple or restaurant maître d' in St. Martin. *Shock for me, discomfort for the receiver. All the subtlety of a falling boulder.*

Is it any coincidence that I threw myself into Jhumpa Lahiri's *The Namesake*, a book about identity?

St. Martin became a week of searching. Over and over I listened to "Both Sides Now" while walking on the beach. I let Joni Mitchell's lyrics wash over me, listening without straining to hear. Cloud images formed in my head, the clouds of my own story. But even as my mind wandered, the words evoked feelings of peace and reassurance.

I even searched for connection at a French restaurant called Rainbow Cafe, where Brett and I first dined before we were engaged. At once the familiarity of the tables—covered by the same blue-checkered tablecloths—and the painted white clapboard walls comforted me. The view hadn't changed either; you could see the whole of Grand Case Bay. The red snapper was still as fresh and deli-cious as I remembered, this time served in a light pesto tomato sauce with a Parmesan onion crust. I felt awkward dining alone, as though customers would pity me being single in such a beautiful place (as if they noticed), so rather than sit through an entire meal of silent, swirling, crystalline thoughts, I was quick to tell the waiter that I had recently been widowed. The young man stood mutely, shaking his head and clasping his hands together as the story came gushing out of me. I'm here now, I told him, because I want to remember.

"Madam, may I bring the owner to meet you?"

Next thing I know the owner invites me to join her for an after-dinner drink. We make friendly conversation; it's so nice, in fact, to connect with a stranger that I decide to dine here again later in the week. What a relief to know that I needn't try to disguise my identity. They already know I'm widowed; next time will be easier.

It would be four years before I ceased using the words "I'm widowed" as a calling card. All this time for me to see that the widow's curse was of my own making. All this time for mourning to metastasize, keeping me tethered to Brett yet away from feeling entitled to live as my own person. Not just widow, but woman, mother, daughter, granddaughter, writer, friend.

No, the world was not viewing me with pitying eyes; I was viewing myself that way.

No Life Insurance

UNLESS YOUR FATHER OR UNCLE OR COUSIN SELLS life insurance, you and your young spouse don't think to purchase it when you marry. Who wants to think about such morbid matters when you are just beginning to really live?

We had no life insurance.

We have plenty of time to start a family and plan for the future because we are still so young.

Yes, we had time to take care of this technicality, but when we finally got round to doing so, it was too late for Brett. He was only thirty-two years old when he was diagnosed, although it wouldn't have mattered had he been eighteen or fifty. *The only proof of cure is life* becomes a sound argument in the context of living, but has no relevance in the cut-and-dried world of insurance. We did, however, benefit from the magic of Manhattan real estate. Little did we know that our apartment would nearly triple in value. That's how I managed to move west when the time came.

I tell every young married couple I meet to buy life insurance. I sound like a parrot. "Polly want guarantees? Buy life insurance." The free advice is just another giveback of loss. Because young or old, parents or no parents, certainty is more an illusion than a warranty. You might as well insure when you can.

Shoes in a Garbage Bag

GEORGE AND HIS WIFE, JANET, CAME TO HELP ME clean Brett's closet. They offered, and I accepted. I had wanted to give George some keepsakes to thank him for being such a true friend to Brett, especially that last year, when witnessing his best friend's unthinkable demise might have kept him away.

Who, after all, feels compelled to immerse himself in the process of dying? Who doesn't fear a twinge of honest reflection: "What if it were me?"

Not George. With four daughters of his own and a demanding job, he made it a priority to visit, staying overnight at the hospital and later at Cabrini Hospice. That last visit at Cabrini, George rallied "the boys" from the University of Maryland, and together they came with cheesesteaks from the famous White House Sub Shop in Atlantic City. I still picture the seven of them sitting in the drab family room, raising the Maryland flag as they shared one last cheesesteak with Brett, a swan song of meat, cheese, and grilled onions. These "boys" were there when Brett and I met, throughout our dating life, at our wedding, and now—was it even possible?—gathered one last time to say, "Thanks, Brett, for everything you've given us. We'll miss you every day."

Pair by pair I removed Brett's shoes from his cedar closet, stuffing them into a large garbage bag. A garbage bag. My husband's life is not measured by the value of his shoes, but it's also true that his shoes grounded him to the earth. And now I discarded them (him?) like waste, into a trash bag. Rubbing my hands along the rough soles of his loafers, this most soulless of realizations made me sob convulsively. Janet, who had been in the living room with her four girls and the twins, heard my cries and came at once to take over the job. Janet is an efficient friend, a model of organization, a cool and detached mourner, unlike George, who on that day, was as distraught as I was.

We got the job done. We cleared the closet. I gave George a crewneck sweater, a Michigan Rose Bowl cap, and a golf watch that recorded the time and score. A handful of items I set aside for the children in decorative boxes—dress and sport watches, three ties, four pairs of cuff links, business cards, a black leather briefcase, a wallet, and Brett's graduate thesis from New York University. And still I placed another small stack of clothes into an undecided pile. These I would deal with at a later time. As for the rest of the clothes and shoes and socks and memories that would never be worn again, George and Janet delivered them in trash bags to their church.

The cedar closet stayed closed and empty for weeks. A few months passed before I gave myself permission to use the space, although not once did I truly claim it as my own. My things may have sat on the shelves, but Brett's empty remains lingered. This was still "his" closet. *Bald and sweet as a peach fixing his tie, giving me a fighting smile.* Some things are beyond rational.

Sunlight

I BARELY KNEW THE FRENCH NEIGHBOR WHO
lived on the top floor of our apartment building, but one day while
getting the mail she randomly asked if I'd like the keys to her apartment. She thought I might like to sit alone on her deck with her
beloved plants while she was at work.

"The fresh air will be healing for you. Come have some tea and
read a book, or just sit."

Her gesture was so unexpected and lovely. It's a gift I accepted
because one thing was certain: I needed plenty of sunlight.

Fragments of a Life

THE FREQUENCY OF THE SYMPATHY CARDS LESSENED over time, but still they came and would continue to lift and heal me. One came from Brett's college friend Tim, who e-mailed him on his birthday, May 26, 2004, when Brett would have turned forty.

Happy birthday big guy. You're the one who showed me how wonderful it is to be completely in love with one's wife as if it were day one all over again. You're the one who helped me show unconditional love to my kids, siblings, parents, and not to let daily hiccups interfere. You're the one who taught me how to enjoy life, how to cherish every moment, and how to fight for every last opportunity to embrace it till our last breath. You're a great guy, Brett. A great husband, a great dad. A great brother and son. And fortunately for me, a great friend. You're an inspiration to us all. Sorry this is so sappy Brett but I've realized that life SHOULD be a little sappy. It's your birthday, Brett, and I really miss you.

No one was forgetting. Friends that Brett had grown up with in Connecticut organized a golf tournament that summer. It was an occasion to bring people together—to remember—and also to raise money for the twins' college fund. They called it the Brett Classic. He would have loved it.

And sometime that spring, George felt that there should be a book of letters for Casey and Rebecca so that one day the twins would come to know their dad. George sent an e-mail inviting people to write about how Brett had touched their lives. The e-mail spread so that a year later, when George had gathered all the notes, photographs, and poems, we had representation from family, friends, colleagues, and distant acquaintances, all of whom cared enough to record their thoughts.

He took nothing for granted, devoured the time with you, adored every moment. He didn't think in those moments, he simply absorbed, breathed you deep, allowed himself the intoxication that only a parent knows for a child.

I will never forget the way I watched my older brother fall in love with you.

He enjoyed talking to me about his plans and trying to teach me how to plan for the future even though he knew I would probably not follow his thoughtful advice. For that, he was a good brother-in-law and friend.

If you find yourself standing vigilant for a belief, even if it's not the popular choice, that's your dad in you. Once, we were at a restaurant and someone at the table snapped their fingers to get the waiter's attention. In a voice I had never heard before, your dad said, "If you do that again, I will get up and leave."

I've known a lot of people in my years in the magazine business, but without question Brett was the most fundamentally decent person I ever worked with.

Someday I will show the book to the twins. When they are teenagers perhaps, or in college, and want to know the story of their father's life.

And the small pile of clothes that sat in a bag at the bottom of his closet? I learned of a woman who quilted memory blankets and asked her to create two small quilts for the twins. "What did your husband love to do?" she wanted to know. Working. Playing golf.

Sailing. Being in the mountains. From this information, she created a quadrant for each passion, using scraps of Brett's clothing as her material—blue jeans, a navy cotton sweater, several striped and solid business shirts, collared polo shirts, T-shirts, and ties. The quilts are identical save for the back sides: Rebecca's is coral and Casey's is romaine lettuce green.

To this day, only the concrete images of the boat, mountains, golf tee, and *Money* magazine logo have relevance for the children. Neither one asks about the clothes themselves, about the memories associated with the navy sweater, the cranberry business shirt, or the Brooks Brothers tie that Brett was so proud to buy himself.

At first, both children slept with the quilts. Until one day I decided to shelve them in the closet, in sealed garment bags. When is mourning smothering? I worried about strangling the twins with sadness, forcing them to remember even though every doctor and counselor and friend who had lost a parent at a young age insisted, "They will not remember him."

The uncertainty over when and how much to encourage their grieving shifts as the years pass. Today, Casey keeps his quilt in the closet—he can stand on his toy chest and pull it down if he wants it—while Rebecca insists upon sleeping with hers every night. "But I have to, Mom," she says when on a few occasions I suggest she not take it to a sleepover. While she never says so, I assume some part of her realizes this is all she has left of her father in the physical sense, his clothing against her skin.

Then and now, these fragments stitched together into matching quilts give a larger sense of Brett. Here is their father and his life, in twenty-eight-by-thirty-inch coverlets.

"When I get married, can I bring the blanket to my wedding?" Rebecca asks one evening in bed.

Let's Go Home

"BUT WE ARE HOME, CASEY. This is where we live."

"No, it's not," he says in a playful, teasing voice, hands on his hips.

We go back and forth like this, relentlessly, until he registers the concern on my face. Is he having delusions? I wonder. Does he really *not* think this is our home, the same home we've lived in all his life? I haven't yet brought him to the psychiatrist, a specialist in grief who had been recommended to us by one of Uncle Harvey's closest colleagues. This incident jump-starts the process.

"Don't worry, Mama," Casey finally says, breaking the cycle of cat and mouse. "I'll find my daddy and bring him home to you." He's told me this before and is obviously stuck on the idea that somehow he has the power to return his father and make our home feel like home again.

I begin to realize that home must be redefined for all of us.

Dysfunction

IT HARDLY MATTERS THAT BY NOW I HAVE SORTED the majority of Brett's clothes. Dysfunction, I come to see, is an after-shock of death that reverberates for years. In the beginning, you are supposed to live in chaos after losing your young spouse because there is nothing ordinary or orderly about the loss. Disorder in your home, disorder in your soul. This is no myth.

The scatterings of the twins' toys, arts and crafts, and sippy cups, these are less overwhelming than the stashes of mail in three different places and the wrinkled Post-it notes and to-do lists written on torn pieces of paper. All that purging and organizing I did a few years ago to prepare for the twins' arrival is defunct. I tend to the basics: I make my bed, dress the children, do the laundry, shop for groceries, and vacuum the kitchen floor at least twice a day because doing so gives me immediate results. Beyond these routine tasks, it's impossible to prioritize. I have no reserves for organizational projects, even those that factor into daily living, like paying bills and returning phone calls.

The trouble is that I don't think straight, and I can't see how to contain the mess around and within me. I'm not ready to grasp at faith since Brett's death, so I dream of kidnapping Oprah Winfrey's organizer, a clever woman named Julie Morgenstern, whose book *Organizing from the Inside Out* has sat on my shelf almost from the time it was published, in 1998. I could dust it off, but instead I Google how to hire one of her people. The idea fills me with equal parts shame and liberation. I feel shame because as a former public relations executive, shouldn't I be able to handle matters in my own home—the sticky cleanup of illness and death? For god's sake, my thirty-nine-year-old husband died in my arms. Shouldn't I be able to manage a little organizing? I feel liberation because I'm practically giddy with relief that someone other than me will take charge.

The silliest thought enters my mind: is this really that different from what my children learn in preschool?

Clean up, clean up, everybody, everywhere.

My Savior Fran

SHE PRACTICALLY FLIES INTO THE APARTMENT. And for once, I welcome the energy. Her name is Fran and she is here to get me organized. The first time she comes the twins are in school, so I give her a tour of the apartment, apologizing for the disarray while pointing out all the areas that need "a home." They are numerous and growing. Like earnest people who clean before the cleaning lady arrives, I'm sure Fran doesn't notice the way I've moved a clump of papers from the living room and kitchen to my office area.

But we don't start in the office. We begin in the bedroom with the cardboard box stuffed with Brett's mail, business folders, and financial paperwork. For months I have willed this box to move on its own, but it doesn't, so now I'm sitting on the edge of the bed watching Fran pick it up in a matter of seconds. She wears an apron stuffed with colored pens. "Let's go, let's do this right now," she insists, plopping the box on the bed next to me. There is no avoiding the task at hand with Fran; I'm paying her and her time is money (mine should be, too, but I'm too foggy to see it this way).

"You can't be vague any longer," Fran says, pressing me to assign each piece of paper a specific category. She leaves me not a second to brew over this insult.

Personal?

Medical?

Insurance?

Kids?

Financial?

In rapid-fire movement she slaps a Post-it on every paper—neat Post-its that haven't been reused and scratched out like mine. One, two, three, she uses her label gun to produce ACTION tabs that program me to do certain things: Bills to Pay, Calls to Make, Items to Discuss with Dad, Things to Read. The best part is that all these action items are tucked inside one ten-by-twelve-inch vinyl folder that opens like a notebook. Fran helps me put everything under its proper tab and then we snap the folder closed with the attached elastic band. Just like that the clutter in my life is contained.

We tackle more than loose papers. At Fran's suggestion, I have my brother, Greg, the architect, design and build a large contemporary storage unit that backs up against one full wall of the family room. This beauty houses all the electronics, videos, DVDs, CDs, cassettes, books, spare platters, dishes, vases, toys, and games. When I close the doors, all I see is a clean, unvarnished surface. It's hard not to marvel at the purity before me.

Fran is a "whirling derby," as Grandma Myrtie would say, but each time she comes back I note how much lighter I feel. We are reclassifying everything (like the CIA only better). I envy her efficiency, I do, and I deal with her intensity and bossiness because the results are self-evident. Plus, she visualizes space in ways that I can't. Not only do I feel productive for re-creating a semblance of order in my home, but suddenly I imagine that I am stealing time. This is no illusion; I think more clearly.

It feels so good to have an uncluttered home and mind that I convince myself Fran is worth the few hundred dollars. "This isn't a luxury," I rationalize, "it's a matter of self-care."

I never want Fran to leave.

I Was Sure I'd Seen Him

EVEN AS THE WIDOW BEGINS TO INTEGRATE THE emotional reality that her husband has died, coming to accept the permanence of death is confounding.

By now I have the twelve original copies of the death certificate that my lawyer father insisted upon, but still, I swear that I've just seen Brett on the crosstown bus. My heart quickens as I catch myself wanting to throw a stone at the window.

"Stop the bus. Is it you?"

A few early mornings he's relaxing on our oversize chair with his feet on the ottoman. By the time my eyes focus and I register the thought, he's gone. Poof, nothing more than an apparition.

My husband is a ghostly presence who never stays put long enough for me to acknowledge the absurdity of these sightings, or my own craziness.

The twins, meanwhile, still think he's hiding.

Stolen Identity

SOMEONE STOLE BRETT'S IDENTITY THAT MAY, using his Social Security number to open a Circuit City credit account and charge $6,000 worth of stereo equipment in two different states. It would have been easy to lift his Social Security number from one of his many hospital visits, or when we refinanced our apartment the year prior.

Stealing a dead person's identity is sick. Beyond the reams of new paperwork and headaches it generates, it is a violent aberration.

Let him be, he's dead already.

As for myself... will it ever end, this confluence of bad things that keep coming my way?

He's dead already.

Casey Buries the Robot

FOR A MONTH I HAVE BEEN TAKING CASEY TO SEE Dr. Ladd Spiegel, the child psychiatrist. He specializes in working with young children who have experienced trauma like ours. While the manner in which both children grieve concerns me, it's Casey who, in these early stages, needs counseling, above and beyond our weekly sessions with Jill.

I give all the love I have to him and Rebecca. But it isn't enough to satiate the hunger he still feels for Brett.

One afternoon in early June, it becomes clear to Dr. Spiegel that Casey refuses to accept the undeniable fact that Brett is dead. He's right. With eyes and body darting and urgent, Casey tells us Daddy is waiting in the hospital. "We need to get in our car and pick him up."

Silence. Neither Dr. Spiegel nor I utter a word.

And then, perhaps because we haven't responded, Casey says, in a more somber tone, "We scared him away."

"Oh no, Casey," Dr. Spiegel answers quickly. "No, no."

But Casey can't hear the truth. He simply runs from the room.

"See how smart he is?" Dr. Spiegel says after this brief performance. I am crestfallen.

We have work to do, that's clear. Dr. Spiegel suggests we reread the booklet Jill created about going to visit Brett at the cemetery. To help stimulate these real conversations I must have with both children, he sketches something that is at once complete and fragmented and chilling on a single page: our apartment building, the hospital, our car, the cemetery, Brett lying in a coffin beneath the ground, and Brett above the clouds. How he captures all of this on one sheet of paper is wondrous; the kids think so, too, because they can't stop staring at the finite, linear map of their lives.

When we come back the following week, Dr. Spiegel gives Casey two small metal robots, one black, one white, and a purple box to house them in. The robots are for pretend play, for Casey to make conversation with his daddy. Casey is fascinated by the robots and immediately begins to play along. Minutes pass with Dr. Spiegel watching before he encourages Casey to bury one of the robots in the box. Casey does the job with great resilience and little drama, and is proud to receive the robots and the box as a parting gift.

My son no longer remembers burying the robot. But once is enough.

Baby Steps

REORDERING THE APARTMENT WITH FRAN HELPS
me see all sorts of things.

With Diane Bell, the financial planner, I create a real budget. My dad goes to probate court, and my father-in-law, Stan, helps me figure out when and how to exercise Brett's options from Time Warner and *Business Week*. Diane insists I purchase life insurance immediately as a precaution. She couldn't be more right.

I feel stress about my financial future, which is sixty-five percent real, thirty-five percent predicated on fear. Right now we have health insurance, but that will end, and I'm concerned enough that I start to investigate other options. I have to provide for my children. I learn from Social Security that I will receive monthly payments until the twins are eighteen. I also receive a small amount until the time my annual income exceeds $11,000. We can't live on this amount, so I either have to seriously ramp up my consulting practice or get a steady job.

The solution comes to me while I'm crouched on the living room rug poring over medical paperwork. I'm chewing my split nails when a friend of mine from Ketchum calls. We worked together years ago and have remained close. She's calling to offer me a job. She now runs the New York office, so she has the authority. Like manna from heaven, the call is a miracle. I'm so grateful that I start to cry on the phone, which is unprofessional, but I can't help myself. "It's good for you, and it helps us," she tells me. We agree to sort out the details later, when I'm ready to start working, but for now she wants me to know that I have a job that will pay me benefits.

Who ever said loyalty was a relic of the past?

The job means that I have to make specific arrangements for child care. Eurita, who had been with us since the twins were less than a year old, came only a few afternoons a week, and much as I wanted, I couldn't afford her more often. Friends suggest hiring an au pair, and I take to the idea at once. An au pair would be more economical than a nanny, but having worked at UNICEF, I also like the thought of the twins being exposed to different cultures. With an au pair, I can even schedule free time on weekends.

Had Fran not helped me order the apartment, I might not have anticipated all that was possible.

I move my office from the spare room to a corner of the kitchen, again relying on my brother to build a desk space. We have two au pairs in that apartment. First, a shy nineteen-year-old from South Africa who needs mothering more than she can help mother. And then, a twentyish, outgoing girl from New Zealand. I depend upon these young women to serve as backup mothers, an unfair expectation in hindsight, but born from the towering demands of single parenting.

What I did not anticipate during our two years living with au pairs was the sense of loss their departures brought. The twins made little distinction between Prelisha and Natalie and family. They, of course, wanted them to stay forever. Away is not the same thing as dead, even though South Africa and New Zealand are too far to visit. *The honest truth. This is what they deserved.*

Who Knew?

ONLY MONTHS AFTER I BEGIN MEETING WITH RABBI Matthew Gewirtz does he tell me how depleted and lost I seemed that first session in June.

At the time, I had never set foot inside Rodeph Sholom synagogue, only twenty blocks south and four blocks west of our apartment, and now, here I am, meeting with one of the rabbis for guidance. In search of bereavement groups, I'd followed a few leads given to me by a social worker who'd counseled me at New York University during the last few years of Brett's life. One person led me to another, and another, and that path led me here, to Rabbi Gewirtz's small study.

I came from the street, as I took to saying. Which, to my amazement, made no difference. This kind rabbi put me at ease with a friendly smile, warm, searching eyes, and the welcoming gesture of pushing aside papers and books at his table to make room for me. He expressed his condolences and right away wanted me to know that there were other young widows in the congregation, women in their thirties and forties who had lost their spouses during the September 11 attacks. *You might feel alone, but we can hold you up* is what he seemed to convey.

In all these ways Rabbi Gewirtz made me feel as though my presence mattered. Most important, he never asked the cliché question I had begun to loathe, "What can I do for you?"

Feeling needful was one thing—I couldn't have been more wanting of faith and time and patience and words and deeds of comfort—but being more specific, and then asking to have those particular needs met was another. *We don't burden other people outside the family.* This was the message of my childhood, passed down from my grandparents to my parents, to me. Brett's family operated the same way. I struggled with this wisdom (countless people had already helped me), so in this moment of unadorned self-examination I chose the Rabbi's path of healing.

I could almost hear the emptiness of my soul as I began to tell him the long, seven-year story. Draining and sad to share, the cumulative quality of the words stretched out over all this time exposed the very thing I felt I should disguise—my cavernous need.

But the widow wants to be listened to.

"So when can you come back?" Rabbi Gewirtz asked me, reaching for his paper calendar. The question stunned me because I hardly expected to be invited back. He was looking at me with a raised pen, and I could tell that he was not going to let me leave without committing to a future appointment.

Who knew that this beloved Rabbi presiding over a congregation of thousands would insist upon setting aside time to speak to a woman with no affiliation to this or any temple?

Who knew that in this urgent, eclipsed time of the young woman's life she would come to view Judaism with a wide-angle lens? Or that through her conversations with him and subsequent talks with his senior, Rabbi Robert Levine, she and her children would learn the true meaning of tikkun olam, to repair the world, one person at a time. She had no idea that a single conversation would allow her to feel more genuinely about her Jewish identity than she might have imagined. And that those feelings would deepen, even as she lunged at whatever strands of faith she could through songs, poetry, conversations with her minister neighbor, the occasional service at Riverside Church, and glasses of wine with her friends. Somehow being Jewish now meant something personal and sacred to her; it was no longer a label or a cloak, but the seed of something sturdy and fundamental within her.

There was just one thing Rabbi Gewirtz asked me during that initial meeting. "How about next week?"

A Few Healing Words on Faith

FAITH IS THE BIRD THAT FEELS THE LIGHT AND sings when the dawn is still dark.

—Rabindranath Tagore

I Kept Coming Back

MANY TIMES I ASKED PERMISSION TO SIT ALONE
in the jewel-toned, vaulted sanctuary of Rodeph, to be with myself in the
larger house of God. As I'd done at the Riverside Church, I loved to sit
on the velvet cushion with my back stiff against the wood pew, my breath
and body the only sounds audible. Anything else—a distant echo, creak,
or rustle—was shrouded in expectant mystery. If God existed, God was
here. In the grandness of this space I felt a sure sense of reverence.

These were new feelings for me, and I liked them so much that
the twins and I began to attend Shabbat services on Friday nights.
For as long as the children were able to sit (each week it changed),
we stayed in the sanctuary; once they got restless, I brought them
upstairs to play, in the company of other children.

I loved the routine of these Friday evenings: preparing a simple
meal for the three of us; dressing in clothes that conveyed thought;
riding two buses to Rodeph so that we could take a taxicab home;
walking hand in hand into the mosaic foyer; and sitting side by side,
one of my arms slung around each twin.

I am still in awe of the way I came to meet a whole community
there, people who had eluded me until Brett's death but who remain
in our lives today. Nothing could have prepared me for the way they
would hold us, and how we would embrace them. We became proud
members. We belonged somewhere. We began to heal.

Two Heads in the Same Executive Chair

I INTENTIONALLY STAGGERED OUR FIRST AU PAIR'S arrival and my return to Ketchum. Prelisha arrived from South Africa tired yet wide-eyed about New York City. She remained homesick for months, keeping to herself in her small room, but was otherwise responsible, so I had no choice but to leave the twins in her care and begin my job.

It was the fall of 2004, six months and spare days since Brett's death. I believed that I was ready to enter the workforce. In truth, I wanted to be *more* than ready. I wanted to prove to myself that I was still capable, and to the entire crew at Ketchum that my loss was nothing to be pitied, that I was hired to bring valuable contributions to the agency. They created a position for me, with the lofty title of Director of Cause Marketing & Strategic Philanthropy. A first for them.

My job was to support existing client relationships by recruiting their corporate foundations and employee relations teams, those areas that focused on giving and civic engagement. I also helped clients partner with nonprofits, like the Larry King Cardiac Foundation, a client relationship I supervised. I worked three full days a week, sometimes more from home. There was limited travel involved, to Colorado to pitch what was then the First Data Western Union Foundation and a few times to Washington, D.C., to unveil the Genographic Project, a program about human migration jointly sponsored by our clients IBM and the National Geographic Society.

The job was everything I wanted it to be—and more—and therein sat the problem. I wasn't ready. I wasn't sharp. I was still, I came to see, a fray of tangled wires on the inside, jumbled and vulnerable. It isn't clear to me what others felt, only that I felt dissociated from myself. Not so much at meetings, because I could still rely upon my interpersonal skills to carry me. A bright smile, a look of curiosity, the seed of an idea. The real challenge came in the administrative functioning, the processes and systems that I needed to adhere to—checks and balances that are integral to any business. The part of my brain that couldn't visualize how to order my apartment—how to purge and cluster files and create efficient space—was the same part of my brain required now to act in a leadership capacity. My cerebral cortex still hadn't recovered.

I'd been a leader before, but for all my past experiences, in career and in life (hadn't I led Brett to a peaceful end?), I could not summon the passion or skills to do so now. What I learned on the job was the opposite of what I was hired to do. In the aftermath of Brett's death and all the new obligations resulting from it, I needed someone to lead me, to take me by the hand and say, "Come. Do it this way. Follow."

Just like our au pair Prelisha, having to navigate her way in a new country and new city, I had to adapt to this foreign way of thinking. For it was never in my nature not to lead. My inadequacy also existed on a deeper level. Had I lost cognitive abilities since Brett died? The idea terrified me. At another time, yes, I could have led with confidence. But now I was seeing double. Literally. Two blond heads in the same executive chair. These are the moments you grip your own chair tightly until the sensation of otherness passes.

Space

HOW IS IT THAT MOURNING ONE PERSON'S ABSENCE
can fill so much space?

The Sky Is Everywhere

IT'S JUNE 17, 2005, OVER A YEAR SINCE BRETT DIED, and I still haven't taken the twins to visit his cemetery. The "Daddy is hiding" phase has passed, or at least they no longer verbalize such claims. Jill still comes to the apartment, and we're still seeing Dr. Spiegel. Slowly, the intensity of the twins' fears has lessened.

Enough so that while driving to my parents' house in Easton I decide to casually point out a neighboring cemetery, just to see the sort of reaction it triggers. The kids are sensitive about all things related to illness and death, and instantly begin to make connections.

Rebecca holds an imaginary phone to her ear. "Hi, Daddy. I miss you," she sings.

She's in a chatty mood and tells Casey that even though they can't see Daddy anymore they can still talk to him. This is language straight from Jill, and an early indicator of the presupposed role Rebecca assumes as the older twin and, hence, big sister.

Casey, however, offers his own explanation. "We can't *see* Daddy because he's in the sky." His tone is so calm and certain that I wonder if he's thought about this before.

I grab the steering wheel harder.

Rebecca is confused. "Is the sky back that way, Mama?" she asks, pointing to what she believes is the direction of home.

Now I'm hypervigilant, thinking about how to answer the question.

But I don't ponder long, since Casey, in the same confident tone, does the job. "No, Rebecca, the sky is everywhere."

The sky is everywhere!

What a startling, perfect truth the twins have decoded: *Daddy is in the sky, and the sky is everywhere.*

I'm so happy that I want to pull the car over and hug them close. I commit to remembering this moment forever.

Years pass before I realize the significance of the date this conversation occurred. June 17 is my parents' anniversary and, quite often, Father's Day. June 17 is also the day the three of us will move west, to Colorado, to begin again. But not yet, that's coming. The point is, the sky is opening for me, I can already feel it.

Was It Contagious?

NO, BRETT'S CANCER WAS NOT CONTAGIOUS, NOT medically speaking. You don't catch brain tumors the way one catches a cold or pink eye. This, at least, is the rational response.

But illness like this is seldom rational. Just when I thought I had accepted that indeed terrible things could happen without cause or explanation, my perspective shifted again when a series of still more terrible things happened within our family.

First, Stan was diagnosed with lung cancer nineteen months after Brett's death. He was the least surprised by the news. When the silent negotiations to take him, not Brett, went unanswered by God, he simply gave up on life. Brett's loss robbed the very life force from him. We all felt that.

Because I could not absorb the pain of watching my father-in-law sear me into his dying brain just the way Brett had, of reliving Brett's cancer, regressing and becoming old in my body and soul, my view of the world foreshortened again by illness and premature death, I distanced myself emotionally. For the twins, too, it was all too much too soon; I wouldn't share the news with them until the last possible moment. Which came only a few months later, in November.

I shivered at the sight of Stan lying in bed, gaunt, drained, hands shaking, the crimson golf hat from the Brett Classic loose on his head. The sight made so sad that I almost couldn't bear to be in the same room with him.

He died at the end of the month, at home with my mother-in-law, who has now buried her husband of forty-three years and her only son.

The only good thing about Stan's death is that he saw his daughter, my sister-in-law, Marcy, marry her longtime boyfriend, Jaime Begian, that September. One happy occasion.

The following year a beloved aunt—the wit and smiles at every family gathering—died of cancer.

And finally, the worst sort of loss. Two young cousins, twenty-one-year-old Joseph, and three-year-old Sophia. Both tragic deaths.

The same family. All these losses. Four years. So, I ask, was Brett's illness contagious on some spiritual level? Or was this simply more voodoo thinking on my part?

The world was suddenly made very small for me. Before Brett's diagnosis, no one was sick or dying. Why were these awful events following us now? And how do you keep explaining the same news over and over to your young twins—*your* grandfather, *your* great-aunt, *your* cousins—when they have already learned that life can be unfair? More than anything, these children need to trust that the world isn't chaotic. Everything in their experience refutes this knowledge, but believing in the order and security of the world is central to how they must live.

My Children Sustain Me

MY CHILDREN SUSTAIN ME IN WAYS I HADN'T FELT before Brett's death. Our love is more ferocious now, more essential. Casey asks repeatedly, "Mama do you need me?" First thing in the morning, midday, at night, the same question comes at me. He's wise beyond his years because he knows the answer is "Yes, sweet boy, I need you and your sister more than anything in the world." No matter how tired or stressed I feel, my son's words lift me. He recognizes this, and is delighted with himself for saying the very thing I need to hear. This is love that cuts across all pain.

On my days off from Ketchum, I pick the children up from preschool and they run at me, shrieking, "Mama, Mama, Mama." They grab my thighs and I lean down to hold them close in a tight, stooped embrace. Our reunion at the end of a school day is loaded with perfect joy and security, and perhaps it's only my perception, but this is not so with the other children and mothers. Everyone is happy, just less visibly needful.

Once, while reading a favorite picture book, *Babar's Museum of Art*, Casey admires a painting of a family having a picnic (it's modeled after Seurat's *A Sunday Afternoon*). He looks longingly at the image and says, "Every day's a special day, Mom." He's right about that, even though I'm not certain he understands at a few weeks shy of four years old what it means to appreciate the day itself. We continue reading, until he stops at a page showing a father in a kelly green business suit. The father is sprawled on a black couch within a jungle. Animals surround him. My squirmy boy is transfixed. He can't take his eyes away from this scene. "I wish we were in that photo," he says to Rebecca and me.

I study his searching face but don't know how to validate his need for our family to be whole again, safe inside a painted world.

We can't help but love differently.

I Needed to Make a Change

THERE MUST BE SOMETHING MORE FOR ME.
This is the thought that grounds me at a time when I am forced to think about my future in New York City. I have no vision because I'm bogged down by kindergarten applications, school reports, and new and increasing job demands. All these stressors are real and normal, but it's the race to land a kindergarten spot that feels like the most daunting obstacle; the task is hard enough for one child, doubly so for twins. This, of course, discounts children who test well and can enter a gifted and talented program, as well as those who draw a high lottery number, warranting a spot at the public school of their choice. We had neither the advantage of testing nor the lottery, which led me, for a short, muddled span of time, to look at private schools. The blurriness evaporated when upon opening an acceptance letter for Casey my eyes darted to a sentence that read, "The annual tuition for kindergarten is $38,000." I crumpled the letter at once. *This is insane*, I thought, beginning to do the math in my head for the next few years alone.

Everything seemed insane to me at this moment, as though our being here suddenly made no sense. The city grated on me in ways it hadn't before: I was fed up with the hassles of daily living, especially the unrelenting noise and congestion of people, cars, buses, buildings. Even the crowded skyline bothered me. What, I wondered, had attracted me to such bustle earlier? On a more philosophical level, I also felt a growing intolerance toward New York City's distorted expectations. This is a city where everyone is climbing some-where—to the next best job, restaurant, school, date, musical, play, art opening, apartment, coop, entire building. We move in vertical increments to survive. That's what the lifestyle requires. But who is really satisfied? And where is the flush horizontal surface to pause and catch your breath?

With my reserves emptied, and something palpable within me craving another way to live, I found myself asking, *Why?* As in *Why am I here?* I'd hit bottom, and while no clear path pulled me forward, I knew that I needed to leave this frantic lifestyle as well as the ghosts of illness and death that shadowed me here. I found myself reflecting heavily upon these last years of caregiving and mourning as my fortieth birthday neared. You can always count on a zero birthday to bring you to the precipice. The more I thought about the lost years, the more sharply my brain focused on change.

Endings. When is it time to say goodbye to the home you've known? When is it time to begin again? Time to move on, carrying your stories with you without being defined by them.

There must be something more for me.

Just Like That

ONE SATURDAY MORNING IN MARCH 2006, MY
college friend Lisa Traeger and I drive to Connecticut to flee
Manhattan. The twins are in the backseat watching *Dora the Explorer*
on DVD. God bless the car's DVD.

Lisa also felt burnt out from work and life. Her job as a magazine
publisher required constant international travel, and she was jet-
lagged yet again. Lisa spent a lot of time with the twins and me this
second year after Brett died. Whenever she returned from one of her
travels, she came for a home-cooked meal, always with a good bottle
of wine. The twins loved her because she gave them piggyback rides,
played Thomas the Tank Engine down our long stretch of hallway,
and nibbled at rubber bacon and eggs from their play kitchen. "These
are the best eggs I've had tonight," she'd tell them, licking her lips
as they ran off to feed her more. She was easy company, and I grew
comfortable leaning upon her because I wasn't taking her away from
a husband or partner.

Besides, Lisa was mourning, too. A German boyfriend, a successful
government minister, had cruelly and abruptly ended their relationship
months before, crushing my beautiful, confident friend. For this reason
she wanted to be with the twins and me; we helped one another heal.

This Saturday morning while on the Merritt Parkway headed
north, I find myself repeating the same rant I'd had with my mother,

mother-in-law, brother, sister-in-law, and anyone else with sympathetic ears. It went like this:

Living in New York City is madness.

I have no idea if the twins will even get into a decent kindergarten.

And then what?

What if our only option is private?

How will I ever afford this?

I can't.

I should move to Italy. Start over.

Really. Life's too hard here.

This time, however, I blurt out an additional thought. "I wish I could move to Denver." At once I recognize truth in these words because my heart twitches and the air is static.

"You can, what's stopping you?"

Lisa knows of my longtime love for Colorado and of the vacations Brett and I spent in Denver. She even knows about the charming house we admired on the corner of Third and Clermont. The house sat across from Cranmer Park and had a trellis with purple clematis growing tall over a white wood fence. "Who's living in our house?" Brett and I joked each time we visited.

"I mean it," she persists, "you can do it."

Lisa is serious, but still I doubt her, which is telling since Lisa is a devout Christian with rock-solid faith, the sort I envy for its transparency. She simply emanates belief in God, and this gives her a peaceful glow. She's got the look of certainty on her face now.

"I can't just pick up and move," I say, shaking my head in defeat.

"Actually, you can." Lisa is my mirror and is reflecting all the longing in my heart.

"Well," I begin to rationalize, "there are my parents and my mother-in-law. How can I take the kids away from their grandparents after they've already lost so much?"

Lisa's not budging.

"I'd have to buy a house. Find new work. Find a school for the kids. Find a temple. Make new friends."

"Okay," says Lisa, wholly unfazed.

As the list of reasons not to move expands, they grow more diffuse, even to me. "But I like my health club. And I have no idea how to mow a lawn or use a power drill."

I check Lisa's unlined face for the slightest trace of concern and see not a hint of doubt. Her trust is unshakable, and through it, I feel my own faith rise bright as the mid-morning sun. Just like that, before we even exit the Merritt Parkway, and with the twins happily munching Pirate's Booty, their headsets still plugged in, I make the decision that yes, I will move to Colorado.

The two of us are practically punchy from excitement.

That's the real upside of change—hope.

Should I Really Move to Colorado?

PROS

Mountains/Sunshine
Slower pace
More balanced lifestyle
More affordable
Julie and family
A big change
Independence
Further spiritual growth
No school madness
Faith now
Dreams
A backyard for the twins
A new life

CONS

Distance from family
Need work
Away from support systems
The responsibility of a house
I don't want to be a burden
Will the twins be traumatized?
Can I make it on my own?
Leaving Rodeph Sholom
But where will they go?
What if we're unhappy?
What if they don't happen?

Stolen Identity Again

THE IRONY IS NOT LOST ON ME. Just as I am about to launch a new identity in Denver, *my* identity is stolen (a cool two years after Brett's). A trio of fraudulent checks and cash withdrawals by phony Nancy Sharps. The ring of fraud takes place in New York and Westchester: $4,200 on May 25, 2006; $2,000 on May 29; $1,500 on May 31.

This is why three days before moving to Colorado I spend two hours at the New York City police precinct on West One Hundredth Street, the very last thing I want to do, under any circumstances. Detective Smith placates me, but we both know that small-scale identity fraud like this is no priority for the city of New York. I want them to catch the thieves—I'm really pissed—but by now, I just want to get out of Manhattan altogether. Chase Bank has already assured me the money will be refunded. *Just let me be. Just get me to Denver.*

PART FOUR

And Now

Flying High

JUNE 17, 2006. No sooner does our flight from New York City's La Guardia Airport to Denver depart than Casey wants to know when we'll be in the sky, above the clouds. The twins have flown only a couple of times, so this experience feels like a fresh adventure. The entire move is one great adventure for them.

Casey looks out the small window with wonderment. Rebecca is in the middle seat, nuzzling me.

"Are we above the clouds yet, Mama?"

"Not yet."

"How about now?"

"Look up and see for yourself, honey," I say, just as the plane moves through cottony air.

"There they are," he squeals with excitement. "Look, look!" Pause. "Now we can be with Daddy."

I hadn't realized he was searching for Brett in the sky. Yet again.

Still with Us

WE ARE HERE NOW, IN DENVER, SETTLING INTO
our new home. I love the long front porch with its view of a neighboring park and mountains, our inviting red door, and carefully
tended garden in the backyard. Our house is in a development called
Lowry; it used to be an Air Force base. The area feels suburban, and
yet it couldn't be more centrally located within Denver.

I want so much for this house to reflect my intentions for the
future that I hire Julie's cousin, an interior designer, to help me
choose paint colors that favor my senses. We pick serene blue for my
office, celery green in the dining room, earthy chocolate brown for
my bedroom. We paint Rebecca's room in cottony pink and Casey's
tree-shaded space in a gray-blue. This is the first time the twins have
their own bedrooms, and they run back and forth for what seems like
hours begging each other to play in "my" room.

What I love about the house is the way we blend the old with the
new. While living in New York, I had paid to store my grandma Myrtie's
furniture, hoping that one day I'd have a larger space to finally use
the walnut sideboard she'd promised me since I was a young girl. The
sideboard is here now, with her sterling silver inside, each fork, knife,
spoon protected with the same thick plastic covering she used fifty
years ago, albeit milky and yellowed with age. The antique beveled
mirror hangs right above, just like it did in her formal dining room.

It saddens me to think about the traditions lost, the way she used to arrange her table a week in advance, the napkins ironed and silver polished and set. She made a feast, just as her mother used to do, so that she could give her family a pleasing memory. "Sit down, Gram," we'd tease. "Eat with us." But she was too busy serving everyone else. I have no such traditions today. Someday I hope I will.

I also have Grandma Myrtie's white, round kitchen table and four chairs, and her bedroom set, which includes a long dresser with a marble top, a highboy chest with brass doors, a vanity chair and cushioned bench. The wood used to be darker, but she pickled it when she moved to Florida for the last cogent years of her life, before her Alzheimer's kicked in.

From my grandma Casey I have a marble lamp that was a wedding gift from 1934. The lamp sits on her graceful walnut end table from Margolis, a fine furniture shop in Hartford, Connecticut, known for its period pieces. I also have a few of her dishes and a wing chair. Even her mother, my great-grandmother Minnie, whom I knew, is represented in my home with an ivory and petal-flowered teapot that Dad tells me is more than a century old. Same as the old cowbell that she rang to summon her five children indoors from the farm in Hartford. Dad remembers her ringing it for her grandchildren as well.

Amid these treasured antiques is a painting of my mother's called *Evolution* that once hung in a museum. At sixty inches high by ninety-six inches long, the painting fills the wall of our living room, which we aptly name the Evolution Room. It's an abstract work, bright and bold with horizontal lines and circular images symbolizing the chain of life. The twins and I do a rain dance of sorts in this room, laughing and laughing as we squeal "E-V-O-L-U-T-I-O-N!"

I buy a new sofa for the family room but use the Tibetan rug Brett and I bought in Manhattan in 1993. Naturally, I've brought our wedding china, our dining room set, and the tall black kitchen chairs. Julie's cousin suggests that I put away the cherry queen bed of ours. Save it for one of the twins, she tells me. She's right. I buy a king-size mattress and feel healthily extravagant for occupying so much space as a single person. I deserve the space, and this is why I've moved to Denver. My closet alone in this house is the size of the dining alcove in our Manhattan apartment.

As for honoring Brett in our new home, we place a mosaic stone tile with his name on it in our garden. The twins select an open, unclaimed spot, and we make a little ceremony before setting the stone in the earth. "Your daddy's here, up above, and inside of you," I tell the twins.

This is what moving to Colorado has allowed us to see: we feel his love everywhere.

So Much Would Change for Us

WE COULDN'T HAVE PREDICTED THE CHANGES in our lives.

Making a Life

"MOMMY'S A ROCK STAR, MOMMY'S A ROCK STAR," I chant to the kids, swinging my arms high over my head. Their bathroom toilet has been running for days, and I have just now solved the problem. "Mommy's a rock star," they sing back to me, hugging my waist. We are own cheerleading squad.

"The chain came loose, that's all, it was easy to fix."

For once.

I don't know the first thing about taking care of a house. The furnace, gutters, water, electrical wiring, plumbing, alarm system, grass, yard. The words are foreign to me since until now all I had to do was call the building's superintendent anytime something went awry. But now I *am* the superintendent, and a house is a lot to maintain. Before we moved, my friend Cate gave me *Good Housekeeping: The Complete Household Organizer*, a fat booklet with tips and note pages to keep a smooth-running home. I've also brought Better Homes and Gardens *Household Hints and Tips*, a do-it-yourself guide for the rare occasions when I might clean my iron, wallpaper a room, and chart frequent flier miles, half of which I still need to transfer over from Brett's name.

Now that I have *really* bought a house on my own, I have to balance my expectations of being doyenne of the home and garden with my stunning ineptitude concerning their inner workings, except the kitchen, which I'd long ago claimed as my domain. I wish I could be like my friend Jen from New York. The dishwasher breaks and what does she do? Reads the manual and either fixes it or hatches a temporary solution. I'm simply not hardwired this way, by desire or ability, and I miss not having a partner to share the responsibility for tending to such matters. "Where are you, Brett?" I lash out one morning when the outlets in the kitchen stop working and a quick flick of the circuit breakers does nothing to restore them. I'm sweaty and late to drop the kids off at school, furious at the panel of outlets and the dented circuit breaker box, and that my husband has left me in this predicament.

In Denver, the tension of yearning to be handy festers because fantasies of sewing curtains and table runners, installing shelves and lights die hard. Dad, bless him, tries countless times to teach me how to use a power drill—he gets me my very own—but it eventually hits me that I really don't want to learn. I have enough on my plate just managing the house, caring for the kids, who are now in kindergarten, and trying to rustle up consulting opportunities with a former client of mine at Ketchum who runs a corporate foundation here.

For god's sake you are making a new life. Take the pressure off yourself. Such self-admonishment frees me to cobble together service providers. Julie gives me names. Her parents give me names. My neighbors give me names. And I've made a new friend, Ellen, who wouldn't you know lives across the street and sews, changes light fixtures, tiles, does her own plumbing, and restores furniture. She and her husband maintain the loveliest garden with a koi pond, spiderwort, Serbian bellflower, echinacea, hyssop, penstemon, and Jupiter's beard. They have colored lights, wire sculptures, and large pots of mint, basil, tarragon, lettuce, and tomatoes. On more than one occasion, Ellen gives me a tutorial on how to care for my garden. "This is a weed," she says, showing me the proper way to yank it loose. "This is not a weed," she continues, lightly brushing a hosta plant. "This is a perennial. This is an annual." I take notes.

"See," I tell my parents one night over the phone, "it's all working out. You don't need to worry."

Close to Heaven

THERE IS NO BETTER PERCH FROM WHICH TO look out at the world than on top of a mountain. "Can you believe we live here?" I ask the twins, high on Ajax Mountain one picturesque fall day. I want them, even at five years old, to understand that the promise of these towering mountains is why we've moved to Colorado. "Go ahead, sniff the air," I say, which sends them into a fit of giggles. They stick out their little noses and inhale the thin air, laughing with each breath. We are a silly sight, the three of us sniffing mountain air. But I don't care how we look because all that matters to me is this: I want my children to feel as alive and hopeful and right as I do living here.

I especially want the twins to know what it's like to be small amid a giant landscape. "You can trust these mountains," I tell them. They haven't a clue as to what I mean—they're still entertained sniffing air—and under no circumstance do I reveal myself. *The mountains don't die.* I kneel beside them, a hand on each skinny waist, whispering first to Rebecca, "The world's yours, honey," and then to Casey, "The world's yours, buddy." Is it possible to stop time?

The kids can't believe that their dad once climbed this mountain, at 11,212 feet. That was the year before he was diagnosed. "He tied a bandanna around his head, strapped on his red daypack (the one we've brought with us today), and followed Rick, Julie's husband, straight up the mountain. I can still taste the sweat I kissed from his face." "Gross," the twins say in unison.

Living in Colorado is like being on a grand adventure. We watch the sunset from the park across the street, hike Boulder Falls and other nearby trails, explore dinosaur fossils, eat the grapes off our vines, ride our bikes to the ice cream shop, and build a family of snow people with carrots as their noses. When the snow falls, we ski. The kids take lessons, and in no time the three of us ride chairlifts and ski beginning trails on Copper Mountain. "Your dad would have loved this," I can't help but say, often. Bags of M&M's and peanuts fill our pockets, and our cheeks blush like streaky raspberries. We are on top of the world, and it is heaven.

Pancakes and More Healing

"I'M REBECCA ZICKERMAN AND MY DADDY DIED."
My daughter reports this to her kindergarten class as if she might say,
"My favorite color is pink." Sometime after, she writes a poem about
seeing her daddy in the sun. Rebecca's identity is all tangled up in
the past, and it's only since moving to Denver that she has begun to
vocalize her sadness and longing. She cries over pancakes, in the
bath with me, and at night just before bed. "Why did he have to die?"
she asks in a thousand ways. And every evening, "Mama, are you
home tonight?"

Rebecca clings tight, and no matter how close I hold her, spooning
her slender body against mine, the two of us tucked under her mound
of blankets, I worry that no amount of love and reassurance can fill the
uneasy hole within her. I'd fill that hole with cement if I could.

Our school principal leads us to Judi's House, a place for grieving
children and their families. The Denver Broncos quarterback Brian
Griese (son of the NFL Hall of Famer Bob Griese) founded the home
in honor of his mother, Judi, who died of breast cancer when Brian
was twelve. This is the first such support group the kids attend, and
right away they are comforted by the numbers. Suddenly, they aren't
the only ones to have lost a father. Or a grandparent. They meet children of all ages who have lost mothers, siblings, aunts and uncles.
The twins love Judi's House because they romp around the game and

music room, mold clay, and dress up. They bang soft pillows and yell and laugh and tell stories. What's not said in this setting is just as significant as what is since the purest part of loss is beyond words.

I meet other widowed women at the parents' group, which convenes at the same time but in a separate space. There's a woman whose husband disappeared while climbing a mountain in France. His body has never been found and she can't put closure around his death. Her boys still hold out hope that someday he'll return.

Almost immediately it strikes me that I am further along in my mourning process than the rest of this adult group. Most of the women and men are grieving spouses, parents, and children who died only months before. As I sit among the freshly bereaved, I realize two parallel truths. I've come a long way since those early months of rocky sorrow, and right now I need to go forward in time, not back. This is a room full of need, and I find it painful. Hands in my lap, I listen each week, careful, in spite of my instincts to help, not to take on anyone else's trauma. One mother is really struggling; she's lost necessary income, her house is a mess, and one of her kids is in trouble at school. Some fierce spirit within me, the same voice that led me to Colorado, tugs hard with the steady refrain, *Be enough for yourself.*

"You're not obligated to attend," one of the group leaders advises me later. So I begin to skip these grown-up meetings because it's the right thing for me. You can't force grief.

What stories this old brick house contains.

One February Day

JUST AS THE SEASONS CHANGE, SHIFTING OUR environment opens up so many possibilities, one after the next. I see how I am central to these changes and this, more than the actions themselves, gives me confidence to continue stepping forward.

So why not write him? is the question I pose to myself after reading about Steve in a magazine featuring Denver's most eligible singles. Peering at the photo, I see that he's a looker: he has a head of neatly coiffed black hair, crow's-feet that warm and widen his eyes, and a chiseled, masculine smile. Just like a darker, younger Robert Redford, says my new friend, Ellen, who is qualified to make such a claim since aside from her skill with power tools and plants, she's a Pulitzer Prize–winning photographer.

But there is more. He, too, has been widowed with two children, now teenage boys. Had I lived in Denver longer, I might have recognized Steve as one of the anchors from the local news, or been familiar with his story, which is widely known. I might have even read his father's columns in the *Rocky Mountain News*. As it happens, I know nothing about this mystery man beyond the two-inch head shot and caption.

From: Nancy Sharp
To: Steve Saunders
Subject: Hello
Date: February 5, 2007

Hi Steve,

You don't know me and I swear that I have never written a letter like this before, but somehow our personal stories compelled me to do so. I saw your photo in this month's *5280* and had read in *The Denver Post* that you, too, lost your spouse to cancer. Sorry about your loss.

My husband died of brain cancer three years ago. I might have followed your personal story in Denver as it unfolded, but we (my five-year-old twins and me) relocated here last summer from New York City in the spirit of launching ACT 2. My college roommate from Northwestern (I studied theater and English) lives here, so over the years I have come to really appreciate all that Colorado has to offer.

Yes, I am single, and also a writer. I freelance for magazines and work as a speechwriter plus write annual reports and other marketing materials. I'm also creating a series of children's picture books, which, of course, is based on our experience. I consider this to be the give-back of loss.

Attached is a photo of myself so that you can get a feel for the woman behind this note. No doubt you will be inundated with admiring women after your magazine debut. But quality counts more than quantity, and something drew me to you as a like-minded, intelligent person to meet. Let me know if you'd be interested in getting together for coffee or a drink.

Sincerely,
Nancy Sharp

The photo is from Marcy's wedding two years ago. I'm wearing a long, black halter dress that we plucked from the racks at Lord & Taylor in New York City. With my hair tousled and swept in a loose updo, bare neck and shoulders, my cleavage is enticing, and I know it.

Ten days later. No response.

Maybe he never received the e-mail? Maybe he was deluged with other notes? Maybe I should resend the e-mail... just to see?

This time he responds within the hour, apologizing for the delay. Mom and Brenda are visiting from Connecticut, and the three of us sit at lunch reading his e-mail. Yes, he wants to meet. We go back and forth with flirty e-mails.

To: Nancy Sharp
From: Steve Saunders
Subject: Hello
Date: February 16, 2007

My plan backfired. I was going to come home Friday night and give you a phone call (I was looking forward to it), but the e-mail with your number is at work. I'll get it tomorrow and give you a call.

You're right about the need to focus on doing some of the fun things in life. It's actually much healthier for our children. The latest from my son Dylan is that he thinks you look like the actress from *Desperate Housewives* (Teri Hatcher, I assume)... and is annoyed that I haven't called you yet.

I'll call you Saturday.

Steve

Bar Talk and Postwar Moments

JULIE GETS A VICARIOUS THRILL HELPING ME prepare for my date with Steve. We settle on pin-striped black capri pants and a sweater set. Just in case, she insists I buy new bras. She knows me well enough to say, "Those old bras are doing nothing for you and you deserve better." If it weren't for her, I'd probably still be wearing decade-old bras stretched thin as decoupage paper. I spend too much money on lacy bras and matching undergarments with Julie, but at least now I feel stylish inside and out, a new me in new clothing. "God, this is fun," Julie admits, a bit conspiratorially, since my dating life is a joint project. Even Rick feels a stake. "We better like the guy she ends up with since we'll probably have a thousand dinners together."

Meanwhile, Steve's son Ryan fits his dad out in a white-collared shirt, sweater, and dark jeans. Ryan loves fashion and has sophisticated taste. Steve is very proud of this fact, and beams when he tells everyone how his teenage son selected the Armani shirt he wore for the magazine's photo shoot.

Steve is seated at the bar when I arrive, a spot reserved for me on the stool next to his. He has an expectant look on his face, and as I approach, a self-conscious smile spreads across my face since I see that he is even more handsome in person. He rises to greet me.

"You look nice," he's quick to say.

"Thank you, you do, too."

We make superficial, meaningless chatter at the bar. "Hi again. It's really nice to meet you. How was your day?" The conversation serves no purpose other than to ease us into the evening. Plus, the nearness of our stools expedites physical contact. Minutes after sitting down we brush knees and skim elbows. "Sorry about that," I say, emitting shy laughter.

I am not sorry.

Nor is he when seconds later he bumps his long legs against mine.

He sips his beer, and I take a slow sip of cabernet sauvignon. I feel giddy in Steve's company and ask flattering questions about his life as a television news anchor. "Do you enjoy being on camera?" *Duh.* He smiles.

"What are the most memorable stories you've covered?" He talks about going to Kuwait in 1991 at the end of Operation Desert Storm, to the Oklahoma City bombing trial in 1997, and to the Columbine school massacre in 1999, where he was among the first media on the scene. "Columbine was complete chaos. There were dozens of wounded kids on stretchers being triaged, and parents, teachers, and people from the community frantically standing by." He tells me how he reported on the aftermath of the Columbine shooting for years, including funerals for the students, memorial services, and the five-year anniversary. "It was difficult not to become personally invested in a story like this one." I read beneath the surface and see the way he worries over his own children.

People recognize Steve. "There's the guy from 7 News," I hear a couple muttering across the bar. I nudge his elbow because he hears the comment and smiles in the couple's direction. He likes the attention, I can see that. "Show me your anchor face," I ask him, and right on cue, he breaks into a smile so wide that the outer edges of his eyes appear to kiss the corners of his lips.

When the bar talk ends, we move into the dining room for dinner. This is when the *real* conversation begins, the inevitable exchange of war stories. His wife, Pamela, died of pancreatic cancer a year before

Brett. She was forty-four years old and waged an uphill battle from the beginning, her death sentence all but guaranteed. At the time of her death, Ryan was eleven years old and Dylan, just ten. "It was a terrible time," Steve says, politely summing up the obvious so as not to depress either one of us. But I'm drawn in, so I press him for details about her death and how he managed to work in the public eye as she lay dying. "How did you function waking up five days a week at three a.m.?" I want to tell him how valiant he was to manage all these responsibilities, but it occurs to me that valiance hardly matters. Valiance did not save Pam, or Brett, or all the other unlucky people in the world who copped a bad deal.

It's his turn to ask about Brett. He's struck by the length of Brett's illness. "We had a big support network, family and friends, like you, everyone was involved."

"What about the kids? What do they remember?"

"Very little."

I give short answers. This is a date, not therapy, and I don't want to cry. I shift the emphasis. "Brett's doctors really prolonged his life." Steve appreciates hearing this since he, too, feels indebted to Pam's oncologist. He begins to tell me how they even consulted a doctor in New York, and I nearly spill my wine upon discovering that Brett saw this very oncologist. We also learn that all four of us likely attended the same Bruce Springsteen concert in the summer of 2000 at Madison Square Garden. And that we know Katie Couric. Steve tells me a sweet story about how Katie offered her support to him and the boys in the months after Pam died since she'd lost her sister to pancreatic cancer a few years earlier. They all had dinner together in Denver, and the boys gave her a bracelet of Pam's that she wore on air for days. She even sent the boys T-shirts and travel bags from the 2004 Olympics.

All this common ground frees us in an unexpected way. We speak the same language, and this means that it's safe to leave the land of illness and death and return to date banter. We talk about Chris Rock, the whims of teenage boys, school for the twins, life in New York City, travel to war-torn countries, my mother's art, and favorite U2 and Springsteen moments. By now I'm on my third glass of wine and am heady with drink and nascent feelings.

Steve feels the same. He kisses me firm and hard right on the street in front of the parking attendants. His lips stay on mine and he holds me in a suspended embrace (just like the Alfred Eisenstaedt photo of the U.S. sailor kissing the nurse in white on V-J Day). I know Steve's a keeper when he cups the back of my tilted head so that I don't fall.

I whisper the first thought that comes to mind. "Wow."

Good night, Steve.

We Understand Each Other

SURE AS YOU KNOW WHEN SOMEONE OR SOMETHING feels wrong, the queasy truth like spoiled milk on the tongue, the same can be said for trusting when a situation is right. I feel such rightness with Steve. The intuition isn't as bold as when I re-met Brett in Hoboken, where I sensed I would marry him from the first date, but I'm older now and less innocent about life's labors.

With each racy conversation, text message, e-mail, and date—and there are so many at first—our connection deepens. We take walks and play tennis in Washington Park. We meander around the Denver Art Museum. We see movies and hold hands in the dark. "I'm thinking of you and your black dress," he texts. "I adore you," the next morning. "Was that anchor smile on this morning's news just for me?" I tease.

The sex is exciting and makes both of us feel years younger. We crave each other day and night, and with Steve, I feel something beyond crush and lust: I feel conscious, alive, safe. I let him hold me tight without worry over exposing the rawest parts of myself because he still wrestles with his own pain. His eyes well when he reflects upon the very difficult moments: when Dylan would sleep beside Pam at night to keep her company; Ryan's rage that his mother, the central person in his life, was gone; and his own benign, misguided guilt that in spite of his expert research skills he couldn't save his young wife.

A few months after we meet, Steve takes me to Aspen. The combination of the scenery (is there any prettier drive than Independence Road?) and the growing love we feel for each other is near magical. *Can this really be happening?* I think. Later, we visit my great-aunt Helen in Taos, New Mexico; at ninety-five, she wins Steve over with her flanken. This is a fatty Jewish dish, but he's a true Irishman and appreciates beefy stews of any kind. Then, in Santa Fe, we walk in and out of art galleries, looking outside ourselves for meaning. Steve asks a lot of questions about my mother's art. "What's her process?" he wants to know. When I tell my mom about his interest in her work, she's a bit giddy.

No matter where we are or what we do together in these early months, we linger when we say goodbye. We hold tight, lucky to have found each other. Words aren't necessary because there is a spaciousness to our relationship that contains all that is unspoken yet felt.

That summer the twins and I travel to Connecticut to celebrate Mom and Dad's forty-fifth wedding anniversary. I hardly expect to feel anxious about leaving Steve, but I do, and it makes me edgy and insecure in ways that I loathe. I stare at my cell phone by the upstairs kitchen window (one of the few spots where I get coverage in Easton) and feel slighted that he hasn't phoned. I'm embarrassed that logic and trust have flown out this small window, airborne amid the maple and elm trees, Dad's homemade birdcages, and the three brazen deer chomping the grass and Mom's flowers. Steve calls when he can, typically while on break during his workday, wholly unaware that his silly girlfriend has wasted precious energy stewing over his affections. By now, I have already snapped at the kids for being too energetic, which upsets them and makes me feel like a bad mother. All is forgiven by the time we finally speak, even though we have short conversations because I learn that Steve hates to talk on the phone.

I can't figure out why I feel so anxious about our relationship. Steve tells me straight out, "My feelings don't change by the hour,

Nancy." He punches the sound of my name for effect. This is my problem, and I need help sorting out these confusing emotions. Back in Denver, I dial in to my old therapist, Jeanne, who practices in New York. Reverse psychology works here because Jeanne channels all her intuition over the phone. "Everything in your experience has led you to believe that separation isn't survivable. But it is, Nancy. And this is what you will learn in this new relationship with Steve: separation, even for a few days or weeks, is indeed survivable."

The complexity of dating Steve—the euphoria, sadness, fear, and longing in one large pot—draws us closer together. Amid such vulnerability, both of us try to more comfortably place the past within the present.

From: Steve
Sent: March 7, 2007
To: Nancy
Subject: Breakthrough

Hi Nancy,

It's 4:48 a.m. on Wednesday. I haven't been able to sleep.

I now get what you were saying the other night about seeing oneself beyond being "widowed." I do feel different. I want you to know that I'm more excited about the future than I am sad about the past, and that's a monumental change. I can't wait to see you again.

No Coincidences

I SEE IT AS NO ACCIDENT THAT I BEGIN TO STUDY Kabbalah at about this time. Each Wednesday morning I gather in a small, unadorned conference room with seven women roughly my age and older. We make an eclectic group with two psychotherapists (one of whom is a poet), a teacher, an artist, an interior designer, a homeopathic physician, a film advocate and community activist. Kabbalah is better than group therapy because we might actually choose one another. The group is led by David Sanders, a psychologist, who is the first Orthodox Jewish friend I've ever made. I want to study with David because I love the way he views the world as a series of connecting links.

"There are no coincidences in life," he tells us. I believe him because why else have I met Steve. David uses my story as an example. "If Brett hadn't died, you wouldn't have moved to Denver. If you hadn't come to Denver, you wouldn't have found Steve." He isn't minimizing Brett's death, he is merely suggesting that for any one thing to occur a billion other things have to transpire first.

One morning David asks us to introduce ourselves. "Pretend you are meeting someone for the first time at a party." I listen to the others, and when it's my turn, without forethought or hesitation, I say, "I'm Nancy Sharp. I'm widowed..." I stop myself. *What am I saying?* My tears come fast and are pooled with shame. I slouch in my chair, burying my face in my right hand. The room is quiet as a sanctuary. No one says a thing even though I feel the heat of their eyes upon me, staring in empathetic silence.

I have come to this painful truth all on my own. How can I really make a new life in Denver if I am still chained to this old identity? *I am more than a widow, dammit.* I am a mother, daughter, friend, writer, lover of life, insatiable reader, curious soul, woman who loves to cook and nurture others through food. And now I am also Steve's girlfriend. As though I've been clubbed in the head, I know in this moment that it is time for me to remove my widow mask, time to dispose of this label that I made a curse, time to realize that widowhood is not a state of being, that it's part of me but not the whole part.

In Kabbalah I learn to see beyond the frame's edge. "Time is indeterminate," David lectures. "When we reach a level of higher awareness, everything becomes a metaphor for living in a more timeless, fluid state." I close my eyes to absorb his words. The sense of continuity feels right to me. This teaching and those about nothingness—*all things come from nothing*—bathe me in calm, connecting me to Brett and Steve and Denver and the notion of home and personhood and infinity all at once. It's what I feel when I stare at the lifelines in my mother's painting *Evolution*. Promise. Renewal.

Family Time

NOW THAT STEVE AND I KNOW WE'RE RIGHT FOR each other, we spend a lot of time trying to blend our families. Ryan and Dylan are a decade older than the twins, so it isn't easy to find shared activities. Mostly, we bond over meals at Steve's house in Congress Park. Sometimes, I cook ahead at home; other days, when I can deal with the mess of pots and pans and dishes in his sink, the overflowing garbage and unloved floor in need of sweeping, I'll tidy up there before making a meal.

I've long held the belief that the way to any man's heart is food, so now I have three men to please. Gourmet meals don't work for this crowd; I learn this quickly when Steve gently asks me to keep things simpler for Dylan, who has noticeably moved chicken on his plate without so much as tasting it. "You mean he doesn't eat sauce of any kind?" This means that even chicken Parmesan is off the table. Forget salmon and mushrooms and turkey chili and pasta with three cheeses.

With the exception of seafood, Ryan eats most everything, but because I so want to please this family, I start to make special meals for Dylan. Kid food like chicken nuggets and pizza and hamburgers. This puts me in a horrible position with the twins, who decide that Dylan's menu is "the best ever," especially the brownies and banana cake and oatmeal–chocolate chip cookies I make every three days. Eventually I smarten up. I don't need to prepare two meals, I can plate Dylan's chicken separately before adding sauce and mozzarella cheese to the rest. The same applies for pasta. I boil noodles, remove a portion for Dylan and toss it with butter, then add marinara sauce to ours. "I don't eat sauce either," Casey tells us. And so, for a brief time, he gets a special plate, too.

The twins are fascinated with the boys. But one thing drives me crazy. Ryan and Dylan, like every teenage friend of theirs I've met, wear their pants slung low, checked boxer shorts visible for all the world to see. I have no idea how they manage to take a single step. "It's cool," Casey says. "No. It's so not cool," I insist, yanking his jeans upright. "But, Mom, this is what teenagers do." He's six years old.

As the months pass, the twins and I stay with Steve and the boys on weekends. This gives everyone a more realistic glimpse of life as a blended family. Short of playing with the few cars and dolls they've brought, or watching cartoons, the twins need to be engaged. They wake early and are ready for breakfast. "We can't wait until Ryan wakes up at noon," they say (me neither). And Dylan has his morning routine of watching ESPN, which means that the television is his from the time he wakes up until breakfast. Even Steve, I see, requires his own space. He isn't used to young children hungry for his attention; he has teenagers who would rather be out with their friends than spend a night at home with Dad.

The twins and I try hard to respect the world of Steve and his boys, but the way they live is unfamiliar to us. We are a house of early risers, early eaters, up and doers. Meals are planned in my home. Laundry gets done. And bedtime for the twins is more or less fixed, because otherwise they're crabby and tired the next day, which is lousy for everyone. On occasion we ask the boys to babysit for pay, but it's clear babysitting isn't their thing. Plus, they never know their schedules. They say, "I don't know" and "Maybe." This means that on date nights, I have to find a sitter, which necessitates advance planning, an uneasy concept for Steve, who prefers the "wait and see" approach. "Let me wait and see what the boys are up to. Let's wait and see what's happening." We squabble because as a single mother of young twins who works from home, I want evenings out. Date nights are my escape. Not so for Steve, who works long, unpredictable hours at the station. He's happy to change into sweats, sip a beer, and unwind in front of the television or with a book.

Over time our fights become less diffuse. They begin to strike the nerve of our relationship—Steve's ambivalence about raising young children again. "This just isn't what I envisioned," he says, eyes on the floor. He doesn't want to hurt me, and he struggles with the right words, I can see this. The compassionate part of me (the widow) understands; he's nearing fifty and his boys are nearing college. But the mother I am is fiercely protective of her kin. "Not fair. You knew what you were getting into." I don't doubt Steve's goodness. He wants to do the right thing. Still, every time we bump along this road, I feel robbed all over again. *Why, Brett, why did you have to die?*

The last thing I want to do is burden Steve. "I will be nobody's burden, and I won't have you resenting the kids," I tell him. We both cry because this is an intractable situation. We love each other, but our families don't quite mesh. I feel the conflict of trying to make the twins older than they are, which creates even more tension. "Maybe we should break up," I say. "Blame the circumstances."

Steve is shocked to hear me speak like this. Ending our relationship is the last thing he wants to do; he's just trying to be honest. In this instance only, I wish he were less honest. "There can be no middle ground here, the twins and I are a package deal," I tell him. "I know that," he says, over and over.

I have my own fears. Can I handle the demands of running a household of six? The grocery shopping. The cooking. The dishes. The laundry. The clutter of mail and school papers and bills and teenage influences on my young children. Steve's happiness. And the darkest worry of all, that god forbid I could lose again. Steve shares this terror. He's already confided, "I just don't know if I could go through it again."

We bump against all these issues on and off for about a year. My friend Elaine sums it up this way, "You have to go through the seasons together." She couldn't be more right. Steve and I met in winter, when everything was aglow. A time of bright lights, shimmer, and ornament. Pure electricity. Wonderment followed us into spring, when we rode bikes over mountain passes, breathing in all that was good in the hilly air. Flowers bloomed and we walked on grass that had renewed itself from earth brown to vivid green. Then summer, and with it, real heat and afternoon showers. What is life? Choices to be made. By fall, the winds blew and the colors of our relationship deepened. We mindfully worked at braiding the loose threads together. Now it's winter again, and as we huddle by the fire, we feel the way we warm each other. We have cycled through the seasons and realized that what's at stake between us matters more than anything else. Steve will stand by me, and I will stand by him. We want many seasons together.

Epilogue

STEVE AND I WED ON AN OVERCAST DAY IN JULY
2008. We married outdoors at Denver's Cheesman Park under the
halo of the Rocky Mountains. All afternoon the crazy wind whipped
my veil like some divine force. My veil nearly caught fire as I tried to
light the unity candle, but everyone laughed. Uncle Harvey officiated.
Ours was a ceremony that accommodated the fullness of our lives,
namely Brett and Pam and the lives and children we created with
them. We borrowed a little from one religion, a little from another,
and we used our own words and Springsteen's recording of the old
spiritual "This Little Light of Mine" to frame the day.

Now we live as a family of six in the house that I bought. Dylan
put up a real fight when it came time to move; leaving his childhood
home felt like a betrayal. "Your mother doesn't live on the walls of
the house," Steve and I told him. "She lives in your heart." It tortured
Steve to see Dylan with such caged-up grief. As if deliberately staying
put somehow kept his mother alive for him, contained and preserved.
The architecture of mourning really is unbounded, because the
opposite was true for Ryan. He wanted only to escape the memories.

So we created a basement sanctuary in my home with two
bedrooms, a bath, and a media room. We gave the boys a hand in

designing their new space, and eventually Dylan softened, even coming to appreciate the newness. It's a full house, and for months the twins think we're having a constant sleepover party. Everyone is polite with one another. Everyone wants this to work. In spite of the rise in household responsibilities, and the inevitability of bumping against one another's space, I am happy. I feel a sense of purpose to my life again, as wife and mother. Steve, too, as husband and father.

I never imagined becoming a stepmother, or having another man raise my children, but sometimes life hands you the unimaginable. Eventually, I think, the steps that define these relationships—as stepmother and stepfather—will narrow. Steve is the only father my twins have known, and already the time with him has eclipsed the thirty-three months they had with Brett. Some days, they'd swallow Steve whole if they could. Which is not to say that they don't still dream of the father they can't remember. It's altogether different for Ryan and Dylan, who possess the gift and burden of memory. They yearn for their mother in the most primal ways. Her scent. Her touch. Her hold. Their longing saddens me. I've never wanted to replace Pam, I wouldn't dare. But I am a kind of mother to the boys, and at eighteen and twenty, they still need mothering.

Weeks before Dylan left for his first year at the University of Colorado at Boulder, I stocked items for his new room: a desk lamp, office supplies, lavender laundry detergent, towels, protein bars, and the requisite bed in a bag. Steve and I had multiple send-offs. "I can't wait," Dylan told everyone with his endearing right-left-right, closed-eye headshake. His happiness about going to college eclipsed our own sadness. The same had been true when Ryan left the nest.

Just like the other mothers I observed on move-in day, I hung Dylan's jeans and button-down shirts in the closet, and stacked sweaters, T-shirts, and shorts on the shelves above the pole. I saw how this day is as much for the mothers as it is for the children leaving home. We intend to leave our imprint, our influence, our love, and we do this under the guise of ordering our children's new world. So that they'll remember the tender way we folded their shirts, hung their robes, cupped their pens and pencils. We want them to think of us when they put their clothes away at night. And we won't say goodbye, leaving them on their own for the first time, until we have created a sacred space, this mother's den.

Such sweet thoughts are lost upon Dylan. I work at a methodical pace while he clusters shirts that he rolls into balls and shoves onto the shelves. I hold my tongue, but when he turns around, some motherly force prevails. Before I can stop myself, I unroll the clothes, separating casual workout gear from shirts to hang.

We play this game a few more times until the room grows very hot. I know perfectly well that I'm deluding myself. Dylan will never adhere to such order. His room at home is chaos incarnate. But I don't care. All that matters is that he knows I've mothered him today.

I'm so engrossed sorting clothes that I'm oblivious to the way Dylan begins to bristle. "I can do it," he says, grabbing socks out of my hand and stuffing them into the (gasp) sweatshirt drawer. Enter a continuing stream of mothers (they also have first-year students on this floor), who gawk at the size of the room. It's true that Dylan and his roommate's space is the largest we've seen. I acknowledge this parade of mothers, politely asking where they're from and what their children are studying, but Dylan stiffens, turns away. He's even more distant from me when they leave. He's practically seething, and I realize that I'm overstepping my bounds. He doesn't say the words, yet I feel them: *You are not my mother. I miss my mother.*

I swallow my hurt and leave the room, but not before spotting a picture frame on his desk wedged beneath a box of Nutri-Grain bars. I lift it up and see the face of his pretty mother, before she got sick. It appears to be the only photo he's brought of our family.

"I'll be back," I say to deaf ears. Steve's still tinkering with a lock for Dylan's laptop and is unaware of the tension.

How normal for Dylan to miss his mother today. I feel embarrassed because, really, I ought to have anticipated this clear eruption of loss. When you lose a husband and father, a wife and mother, you come to expect milestones like the start of school, birthdays, vacations, and holidays to jolt pathways of mourning. The intensity lessens as the years pass, but the porousness of loss remains. Speak nothing of the subtler reminders like cowlicks, skinny toes, and horses.

Seeing takes time. It's only now that Dylan's on the verge of returning home after a year away that a fresh idea of motherhood is germinating in me. *There can be many mothers.*

Clumsy moments are inevitable in a blended family like ours. Passion for the mother the boys remember, longing for the father the twins never knew. The past lives among us, always, in obvious, layered, and sometimes unexpected ways. Brett and Pam are simply part of who we are today.

Once, I was walking in Riverside Park with my old minister friend, Erik Kolbell, while back East. I'd lived in Denver over a year and had met Steve, but we weren't yet married. Erik posed the question "When things happen, how do we redeem them?" Like the opening line of a sermon, the question silenced me. Erik didn't necessarily want me to answer him, that much was clear. And I was relieved, because at the time, I had no words.

Only now, nine years after Brett's death, and in a second marriage and family dynamic, can I answer this question with the sort of nuanced response it merits. *When things happen, how do we redeem them?* Some things are beyond redemption, I think. How, after all, do you redeem a person's life? It's just not possible to balance the scales after a crushing loss. And yet, human beings are not beyond rededicating themselves to life. To moving forward and adapting. Had I remained stuck in the tragedy of Brett's death, I might not have moved to Colorado. Or risked loving again. Or been able to place my experience within the broader whole, without allowing it to define the present day. I believe this is what it means to memorialize a loved one: to choose life. With Steve, I have learned to sanctify all that is misshaped and broken in the world, making it a part of our story but not the whole part. The veil I wore at my first wedding and the veil I wore at my second wedding flow together. Beauty exists in this transparent, diaphanous space. With Steve, I see the unflinching light of every day.

Discussion Questions for Book Groups

1. Why do you think the author chose *Both Sides Now* as the title of her memoir? In what ways does the author use the phrase as metaphor? In what ways does "both sides now" apply to your own life?

2. What purpose is served by interspersing the second and third voices in this work? At what point does the author shift between the two, and why do you think she makes this choice?

3. The author deliberately wrote the memoir in short, fragmented chapters. What larger message is she trying to impart through this structure?

4. *We go where we need to go.* Does the memoir make you think differently about illness and mourning? If so, how? Have there been moments when coping has altered your perception of reality, or the way a loved one views reality? Did time alter your perspective?

5. At several points, the author questions her own voodoo thinking— the false sense of power she exerts over her husband's well-being. *If I think the worst, it could happen.* Conversely, *positive thoughts breed only positive outcomes.* How have you learned to balance overtly negative or optimistic thoughts when things happen that are beyond your control?

6. This is one woman's story, and yet the book is filled with universality. How?

7. Courage exists on many levels in *Both Sides Now*. What are the most obvious examples, and how is courage shown in more subtle ways?

8. The author takes unmistakable risks in this memoir: having children after her husband's initial cancer diagnosis; moving across the country on her own to start a new life; pursuing a widowed TV news anchor in Denver. What is your comfort level with risk and uncertainty? Under what circumstances could you conceive of recasting your life?

9. How do you think the author views faith? Are her views clear-cut? What about yours?

10. How is beauty juxtaposed with darkness in *Both Sides Now*?

Nancy Sharp is available for book group discussions and appearances. To find out more, e-mail her at *Nsharp@NancySharp.net*.

Where to Turn for Support

AMERICAN CANCER SOCIETY
http://www.cancer.org/

STAND UP 2 CANCER
www.standup2cancer.org

NATIONAL HOSPICE AND PALLIATIVE CARE ORGANIZATION
(NHPCO)
http://www.nhpco.org/templates/1/homepage.cfm

HOSPICE INTERNATIONAL
http://hospiceinternational.com/

NATIONAL INSTITUTES OF HEALTH END OF LIFE SITE
www.nlm.nih.gov/medlineplus/endoflifeissues.html

NATIONAL FAMILY CAREGIVERS ASSOCIATION
http://www.nfcacares.org/

LIVESTRONG FOUNDATION
www.livestrong.org

MY LIFELINE.ORG CANCER FOUNDATION
www.mylifeline.org

Especially for Children

THE DOUGY CENTER: THE NATIONAL CENTER FOR
GRIEVING CHILDREN & FAMILIES
http://www.dougy.org/grief-resources/how-to-help-a-grieving-child/

CHILDREN'S GRIEF EDUCATION ASSOCIATION
http://childgrief.org/childgrief.htm

Acknowledgments

Where to begin?

There are so many people I'd like to thank for their part in seeding *Both Sides Now*. Many of you were part of the up-front story—you lived the events with me by offering strong shoulders and daily support. Others processed the experience from afar, never remaining too distant or emotionally detached. You called. You wrote. You made trips to visit us. You came to say goodbye.

Together, you helped the twins and me heal. After a decade spent caregiving and mourning, you celebrated our move to Denver and cheered when I serendipitously met and married Steve. You are my family, my friends, my former colleagues, my writing community, my rabbis and ministers, my New York City and Colorado worlds.

I wish that I could name every person who factors into this story, but that would be impossible. For those who don't appear in the pages of the book, please know that your untold kindnesses will never be forgotten. You have shaped me into a better person and writer.

I would like to thank:

—My parents, Ron and Sue Sharp, for always wanting the brightest path for me. Never have you held me back, even when it meant leaving for Colorado.

—My mother-in-law, Brenda Zickerman, and father-in-law, Stanley Zickerman, of blessed memory, for their unconditional love since the beginning.

— Uncle Harvey for making everything in life better, even the hard stuff.

—Greg and Marcy for being lifelines, then and now.

—My second in-laws, Dusty and Anita "Nini" Saunders, and all the Saunders siblings for embracing the twins and me as you have. Nini, you are my first reader every time.

—Ryan and Dylan for making my life fuller.

—Harrison Candelaria Fletcher, Diane Hume George, Suzannah Lessard, Madeleine Blais, and Richard Todd for making me a more authentic writer. Thank you for your unwavering belief in me and this project.

—Susan M. S. Brown for your attentive copy editing. Never did I fear and love the red pen this way before.

Finally, for my husband, Steve Saunders, who understands, as I do, what it really means to love and lose and risk love again. Steve, I'm so grateful that I took a chance on you, and that you responded. What amazing fortune to have discovered a way to hold the past while living the present—*our* present.

Published by Books & Books Press
www.booksandbooks.com

Publishing Consultant Ausbert de Arcé
Creative Director Petra Mason

Cover: Homage © Mason
Photograph: © Marcel Botha
Cover and Interior Design: Kaile Smith

Both Sides Now / Nancy Sharp

Library of Congress Control Number: 2013937773

First Edition

ISBN: 9780983937869